THE DEATH OF CIVILITY AND COMMON SENSE

THE DEATH OF CIVILITY AND COMMON SENSE

HOW AMERICA HAS BECOME DANGEROUSLY POLARIZED

Mike McLeod

Published by Gatekeeper Press

3971 Hoover Rd. Suite 77

Columbus, OH 43123-2839

ISBN: 1530227828

eISBN: 9781530227822

Printed in the United States of America

--A house divided against itself cannot stand--
Abraham Lincoln

Dedication

This book is dedicated to Hubert Humphrey, the greatest and most courageous man I have ever known. He was not the man who brought me to Washington and gave me an opportunity to work in the Senate. That was Herman Talmadge. Without Talmadge offering me a job that allowed me to work my way through law school, as well as a job in his office upon graduation, I would never have met Humphrey.

Talmadge taught me to be courteous, conscientious, and honest in all my professional dealings.
Unfortunately, he was undone by a Greek tragedy I would not have believed. That is addressed in the Appendix of this book.

This book is dedicated to Humphrey because he personified the message that this book is written to convey. He was the "happy warrior" who constantly practiced "the politics of joy". He never made things personal, even when he was passionately debating an issue. He was always courteous and respectful of his fellow man. Some referred to him as "the orator of the dawn".

Nothing more starkly illustrates the character of Humphrey than his death. In the morning of January 3, 1978, I was startled to get a call from him. I snapped to attention when I heard his raspy voice on the phone. "Mike, I want you to get me some new material, like the stuff you used to give me. My staff is just giving me the same old stale material. We have a lot of work do to." I said, "Yes sir, Senator, I will get right on it".

I was baffled. I had known Humphrey was in the hospital battling cancer. I had not seen him in quite a while.

On January 13, Humphrey died at his home in Waverly, Minnesota. I later found out he called a number of old friends in the week before he died.

He even called his old nemesis, Richard Nixon, and invited him to his funeral. And Nixon did come, the first time he returned to Washington since he left in disgrace. I heard later that Humphrey even went around his hospital ward cheering up other sick patients.

After Hubert Humphrey died in early January 1978, his body lay in state in the Capitol Rotunda. He was the 22nd person in American history to be saluted that way. Vice President Mondale delivered a powerful eulogy in the Capitol, "He taught us all how to hope and how to love, how to win and how to lose. He taught us how to live, and finally, he taught us how to die."

I know of no other man who had this much courage and grace while he was dying.

One of my goals in this book is to encourage the republication of Humphrey's autobiography in Kindle format, so that his timeless message and his politics of joy can inspire more people today, as well as future generations. One of the chapters in his book is particularly apt for the problems of today. It is "Compromise is not a dirty word".

Norman Sherman, a former Humphrey aide, wrote a beautiful afterword that was published in 1991 in the paperback version of Humphrey's 1976 book, "The Education of a Public Man". He described the thousands of people who filed past his coffin for a day and night to pay their respects. They included the older blacks, who came because he had been a champion of civil rights. They included union leaders because of his advocacy of the causes of working men. Also, they included Senators, Congressmen, and Congressional staff like me who had been inspired to work in public service because of him.

Another testimony to Humphrey's great humanity is mentioned in his book, "The Education of a Public Man". He told of his troubles in fitting in when he first came to the Senate in 1948. He overheard Senator Richard B Russell of Georgia say to some Senate colleagues in a loud voice meant to heard by him, "Can you imagine that the people of Minnesota would send a damned fool like him to the Senate".

Humphrey's book conceded that Russell was the ablest and most powerful of the Southern senators. When Russell died in 1971, Humphrey went out of his way to fly to Georgia and attend Russell's funeral.

Contents

Why I wrote this book

This book is timely because we are now enduring yet another presidential election campaign.. The country is more bitterly divided than at any time in my lifetime. Never has there been a nation political campaign where any leading candidate has been as bombastic and insulting as Donald Trump. However this election ends, the nation will be even more divided when it is over.

Trump is unique in the annals of Presidential politics. Unlike other people who are genuinely rich, he delights in saying "I am very rich" or "I have a lot of money". He is very well known, because of his successful television reality show, "The Apprentice", where he delighted in saying "you're fired".

Trump had threatened to run in previous presidential elections but never did so. However, he was given a chance to express his opinions on everything on Fox News, which is favored by conservatives. He did not have to even show up for an interview. He simply called in on a regular basis and gave his commentary. This is why his behavior in the first Republican debate was so bizarre.

That debate was moderated on August 6 by Megyn Kelly, who has a very popular news show, "The Kelly File", on Fox News. She asked him some tough questions on his misogynistic comments about women. This was his response, in an interview by CNN's Don Lennon:

"You could see there was blood coming out of her eyes," he said. "Blood coming out of her wherever."

Trump them followed up by expressing his displeasure with Fox News in general. After having received a free platform from Fox for years, he boycotted Fox News on the next Sunday talk shows.

Trump has continued his insults of people he doesn't like, such as immigrants, other candidates, and people with disabilities. He continued his assaults on women by dismissing Carly Fiorina by saying "Look at that face. How can you vote for that?" He made fun of perhaps the most respected conservative political commentator in the nation, Charles Krauthammer, by saying, "The guy can't even put his pants on". (Krauthammer has been disabled since a swimming accident he suffered in medical school.)

Trump is the first candidate in memory who has made frequent use of the F bomb.

As bad as things have become in the current Presidential campaign, they have become almost as bad in many congressional races, which occur every two years. Even Senators, who are elected for 6 year terms, must immediately start raising money to pay off campaign debts and build a war chest for the next election.

The process of gerrymandering congressional districts is a practice that adds to disenchantment with the system. This practice was described in a March 1, 2015 article in the Washington Post by Christopher Ingraham, "How to steal an election". He explains "Contrary to one popular misconception about the practice, the point of gerrymandering isn't to draw yourself a collection of overwhelmingly safe seats. Rather, it's to give your opponents a small number of safe seats, while drawing yourself a larger number of seats that are not quite as safe, but that you can expect to win comfortably."

This practice has added to the cynicism of American voters. It is an old practice that has been worse by the computerization of our voting rolls. With computers, it is easy to determine exactly how every small precinct and voters in every zip code have voted in the previous elections.

However, gerrymandering does not happen in the Senate, where every state gets two Senators. In many States, the electorate is either so red (Republican) or so blue (Democratic) that the incumbent only needs to worry about challenges within his own party. I will describe three cases in the senatorial races of 2014 that illustrate this problem. One was an incumbent Democrat and two were incumbent Republicans.

The first example is Senator Max Baucus of Montana, who was the Democratic Chairman of the Senate Finance Committee, the most powerful committee in the Senate. Despite the fact he was in his early 70's, he looked as hale and hearty as ever. I was inspired by him because he had always been an avid runner who inspired me to run and be fit.

Baucus was not having any problem raising enough money for reelection. Nor had he ever had a problem being reelected. However, he had served in the Senate 36 years and knew his constituents. His support had been indispensable to the Senate's passage of "Obamacare", and he understood how unpopular that was in Montana. Rather than face an increasingly Republican electorate in his state, he declined to run for reelection. President Obama appointed him Ambassador to China.

The same thing happened to Senator Saxby Chambliss. He had a good career in the House and Senate, part of it as Chairman of the Senate Agriculture Committee. He was also the Ranking Republican on the Senate Intelligence Committee. In both committees there is more of a tradition of bipartisanship than in the Senate at large. He was a moderate conservative Republican who represented an increasingly Republican state.

However, Chambliss was threatened by tea party elements in his state in 2014. He had been able to work across the aisle with Democrats to get things done. In doing so, he got in trouble with people like Grover Norquist, whose organization, Americans for Tax Reform, tried to force all Republicans to sign a no-tax pledge. The pledge even included votes to close tax loopholes and limit deductions.

Chambliss was only 69 and in good health. That may be retirement age for most people, but it is not in the US Senate. Many of them serve well into their 70's and 80's and some of them, like Robert Byrd, into their 90's. Chambliss declined to run for reelection and retired. He is now working for a major Atlanta law firm.

Chambliss's retirement made this an open seat. The real contest in state wide races in Georgia is in the Republican primaries. Congressman Jack Kingston from Savannah waged a spirited and well-funded campaign. He was a friend of mine, so I helped in his campaign as much as I could. However, he could not shake the perception that as a congressman he had been a part of the problem. In a very close race, he was defeated in a run-off by Tom Perdue, a very successful businessman who had lived out of the state most of his career and never held elective office.

In the general election Perdue handily defeated Michelle Nunn, the daughter of former Democratic Senator Sam Nunn, who is still highly respected in the state.

Other moderate conservative Republican Senators have not been spared challenges from the right from radical tea party candidates. Senator Thad Cochran of Mississippi had served his state for 42 years. I remember that when he was a first term senator he told me why he had joined the Republican Party. He explained he felt as a young man that the Democratic Party in Mississippi was too racist. As the chairman and ranking member of the Senate Appropriations Committee, he had been able to direct millions of dollars to help his state, which is one of the poorest states in the nation.

The Senator faced a very tough race in the Republican primary in 2014. A tea party candidate named Chris McDaniel was endorsed by Sarah Palin and Rick Santorum, as well as several right-wing groups. McDaniel mounted a ferocious campaign which overstepped the bounds of decency by sneaking into a nursing home to photograph Cochran's wife, who had been ill for many years. Even so, he forced Cochran into a run-off. Ultimately, some of his tactics were so extreme that it turned many of the voters off. In a recount, Cochran won by 7,000 votes.

In another high profile race, Republican Senator Pat Roberts had the race of his life. His race received a lot of national press coverage because it was thought that the control of the Senate would hinge on the outcome. The tea party candidate was a radiologist named Milton Wolf, who had posted photos of the skulls of his patients who were gunshot victims on Facebook.

Roberts did overcome the tea party challenge in the Republican primary only to face a challenge from a bogus "independent". The Senate Democratic leadership persuaded the Democratic candidate to withdraw, and recruited a wealthy young man named Brad Orman to run as an independent. Orman refused to say which party he would caucus with if he was elected. However, a PAC controlled by the Senate Democratic leadership donated one and a half million dollars to his campaign.

A few of his Washington supporters such as I went to Kansas to organize some of our clients into campaign events for Roberts. Ultimately, voters of Kansas did not buy Orman's claim to be "independent", and Roberts won by 10 points in the general election.

The American public is the victim of this hyper partisanship and extremism on both the left and the right. This constant political infighting and attacks against politicians of the other party are entertaining to a point. However, this quickly grows old. The essential work of our Republic doesn't get done. The voters are disgusted and tend to say, "A pox on both of your houses".

This explains why voters seem to favor outsiders who have no government experience. Ironically, voters would not trust people with no experience with their personal medical care. They would not even trust someone with no mechanical experience with their automobile. Yet, they seem willing to turn over to someone totally inexperienced in government the toughest job in the world, the Presidency of the United States!

Another oddity in our current political process is the fact that it violates the principles of human conduct. In business, local government, or even ordinary relations with one's neighbors, we don't heap verbal abuse on each other. If we did, there would be even more cases of people shooting and killing each other.

Yet we increasingly do this in our national politics. And we wonder why our government doesn't work!

The purpose of this book is to describe, from my own experiences, how we can pull back from the brink of this polarization and adopt a policy of moderation that would make us a stronger nation.

Since there is no magic formula to solve polarization, I will do so by describing politicians

I have known. The examples cited here come from my time directing the staff of a major committee in the Senate in the 1970's, my involvement in four presidential campaigns, and working on numerous congressional and senatorial races over the years. While I never ran for office, I have great respect for those who do. As that progressive Republican President, Theodore Roosevelt, once said:

"It is not the critic who counts; not the man who points out how the strong man stumbles, or where the doer of deeds could have done them better. The credit belongs to the man who is actually in the arena, whose face is marred by dust and sweat and blood; who strives valiantly; who errs, who comes short again and again, because there is no effort without error and shortcoming; but who does actually strive to do the deeds; who knows great enthusiasms, the great devotions; who spends himself in a worthy cause; who at the best knows in the end the triumph of high achievement, and who at the worst, if he fails, at least fails while daring greatly, so that his place shall never be with those cold and timid souls who neither know victory nor defeat".

While I have always been more of a lawyer and policy wonk than a political operative, I am not as much of a policy wonk as Cass Sunstein. He has written an excellent little book on the subject of polarization of America, "Going to Extremes--How like Minds Unite and Divide". This book explains that we tend to associate only with people who share our political opinions and biases. Therefore, we are mutually reinforcing, pushing conservatives to be more conservative and liberals to be more liberal.

Sunstein served in the first two years of the Obama Administration as director OIRA in OMB. The Office of Information and Regulatory Affairs (OIRA) is a statutory part of the Office of Management and Budget within the Executive Office of the President. This is the division that oversees the regulations that are issued by the Administration.

I got to know him because he was a presidential nominee who had to be confirmed by the Senate, and his confirmation was delayed for several months. He had written a book on animal rights that offended the livestock elements of the agricultural community including my clients in the egg industry.

Suddenly, I was receiving calls from previous budget officials in Republican administration. They told me the guy was a good appointee, and would do a good job of cutting excessive government regulations. I then figured out that they thought I was trying to block his confirmation. They assumed this because of my friendship with Senator Pat Roberts and other members of the Senate Agriculture Committee.

I got a call from Sunstein and he invited me to his offices in the Executive Office Building adjacent to the White House. We soon became friends, and he was confirmed. I hated to see him return to his position at Harvard University after two years. He could have taught the entire Obama Administration how to decrease the polarization of America.

Robert Byrd: The Keeper of Senate Rules and Decorum

As a young man, I was greatly attracted to politics and public service. As I went through law school, I could not imagine that I would like private practice. The prospect of spending my career simply being a pleader for special interests had no attraction for me. My interest was always in government, history and constitutional law.

Next to Talmadge and Humphrey, Robert C. Byrd had the most impact on me. My favorite law school course by far was when Senator Byrd would come out to American University to teach a course in legislative process every Saturday of one semester. He even had guest speakers come in. One was Doc Riddick, the Senate Parliamentarian. Another was his friend, the lobbyist for the coal industry in West Virginia.

Later, when I went on the floor with Chairman Talmadge of the Senate Agriculture Committee, Majority Leaded Byrd would go on the Senate Floor to praise me as one of his best students. This did wonders for my self-esteem. Moreover, when Byrd later faced his only tough race for reelection against a guy named Cleve Benedict, I was the only one he knew in the agricultural community, and I did everything I could to help him.

Byrd later wrote a large volume on the history of the U.S. Senate from 1789 to 1989 and favored me with an autographed copy with my name engraved on the front. The book had its origins when Byrd did a series of lectures on the Senate floor. I have kept it on the coffee table in my office ever since.

Byrd also found time to deliver a series of lectures on the history of the Roman Senate. He would say he loved to study history because, while governments have changed over the years, human nature did not. I grew up from boyhood with a love of history, and this was an extra incentive for me to study history throughout my life.

Byrd also loved the Constitution, and he always kept a little pocket Constitution with him on the Senate floor. I learned more about Constitutional law from him than I learned in a course solely about that in the law school. The difference was that the Constitutional law professor had never practiced law nor served in government. I learned nothing from him. Byrd had served the government since he first ran for office as an uneducated young man who was elected to the West Virginia legislature in 1947.

Byrd was the keeper of the Senate traditions of order and civility. He was completely bipartisan in this regard. He would spend hours on the Senate floor sitting with freshman senators of both parties. He would explain to these newcomers how to be courteous and respectful of their colleagues. He explained to them that this is why when Senators speak on the Senate floor they refer to each other in the third person, such as "the Senator from New York" or "the Senator from Georgia" I have seen Byrd rush over to the side of a junior Senator to plead with him privately to show restraint if he was not following this tradition on the Senate floor.

While Byrd served as Senate Majority Leader 1977-81, and as Senate Minority Leader 1987-89, he continued to study history. He also served several terms as Chairman of the Senate Appropriations Committee. One of Byrd's favorite sayings was that the House was like the cup where the hot tea was poured and the Senate was the saucer where it was poured out of the cup to cool. He meant, of course, that strong passions aroused in the House of Representatives could be calmed by the more deliberate and thoughtful Senate.

On December 20, 1995, Byrd took the floor to deliver an oration on "civility in the Senate." He dressed down the then-Sen. Rick Santorum, R-Pa., who is, like Sen. Ted Cruz, a 2016 presidential candidate. The previous week, Santorum had said Democrats in the Senate, as well as the Clinton administration, were lying about Republican budget proposals.

"I have never heard that word used in the Senate before in addressing other senators. I have never heard other senators called liars. I have never heard a senator say that other senators lie," Byrd said, having already served for 37 years. "The use of such language on the Senate floor is quite out of place, and to accuse other senators of being liars are to skate on very, very thin ice, indeed."

"The bandying about of such words as liar, or lie, can only come from a contumelious lip, and I for one, who has been honored by the electorate to serve in the high office of United States Senator, to engage in such rude language arising from haughtiness and contempt, is to lower himself in the eyes of his peers, and of the American people generally, to the status of a street brawler," Byrd said in a speech mixing history and mixing history with biblical references.

Apparently, Byrd was not on the Senate floor when one Senator Daniel Patrick Moynihan slugged Senator Kit Bond. Moynihan had an amazing career before being elected to the Senate from New York. He had the distinction of serving in the administrations of four quite different presidents, Kennedy, Johnson, Nixon and Ford. Moynihan was a respected intellectual and noted sociologist. Perhaps his most famous statement was one made in a memo to then President Nixon in 1970,"The time may have come when the issue of race could benefit from a period of benign neglect".

My only personal exposure to him was once when he came up to the Senate to talk to young legislative assistants. I seized the opportunity to ask him about a favorite legislative proposal of my boss, Senator Talmadge, and I. We were trying to enact the Senator's bill to provide a tax credit for job training. Moynihan responded that the Nixon Administration was opposed to it because it would wrong to use the tax code for purposes other than the collection of revenue. Fortunately, Talmadge was able to get the legislation approved by the Senate Finance Committee and enacted into law as a part of a larger tax bill. A later version of it is still in the law today.

Moynihan was a hard drinking Irishman. When he became a Democratic Senator from New York he was a strong advocate for New York's interests in the Senate. On one occasion he allowed his advocacy to escalate into a physical attack. Senator Kit Bond, nearing retirement in 2010, recalled with some embarrassment that Moynihan had once "slugged him on the Senate floor" after Bond denounced an earmark Moynihan had slipped into a highway appropriations bill. Some months later Moynihan apologized, and the two occasionally would relax in Moynihan's office after a long day to discuss their shared interest in urban renewal over a glass of port.

I don't know this for a fact, but I feel sure that Byrd heard about this terrible breach of Senate decorum and urged the two Senators to patch it up. For an excellent biography of Byrd see "The Last Great Senator, Robert C. Byrd's Encounters with Eleven U.S. Presidents" by David A. Corbin. It is available on Amazon in both print and Kindle.

Certainly Byrd was not around when freshman Ted Cruz got on the Senate floor to call the Majority Leader of his own party a liar. As reported by the Washington post on Jan, 24, 2015, the Texas Tea Party star made his own bid to force his way back into the national conversation by doing something almost unheard-of in the stodgy Senate chamber: He stood up and called a fellow senator a liar. And not ust any senator, but the leader of his own party.

Hubert Humphrey the Happy Warrior

Years later, I became close to a great American who had served as Senate Majority Whip (the number two position) in the Senate leadership. He then served as Vice President under President Lyndon Johnson after the Kennedy assassination. He lost his campaign for the Presidency to Richard Nixon by a very narrow margin. I always thought that he would have won if he had come across on television as well as he did in person. When he was speaking to a crowd, especially a crowd of young people, he could hold them at rapt attention for an hour. He was not nearly as impressive on television.

However, the real reason he lost was inescapably tied to Johnson's prosecution of the war in Vietnam. The nation was bitterly divided by the war in Vietnam and was ready for a change. My own generation was very much against it. Some fled to Canada. Others joined the National Guard and were called to active duty in Vietnam.

I avoided serving in Vietnam only because I was called to active duty in the National Guard In the riots in Washington, which began immediately after the assassination of Martin Luther King on April 4, 1968? I happened to be attending the annual Democratic fundraising dinner at the old Shoreham Hotel where Vice President Humphrey was the featured speaker. When we sat down for dinner, Humphrey arose to announce that Martin Luther King had just been shot in Memphis.

Humphrey called off the dinner, and I stood around for a while to listen to him talk to the press. Then I left and went to my apartment, where I knew a call would be waiting. I took off my rented tuxedo and put on my army fatigues.

I got to know Humphrey later when he returned to the Senate in 1971 and secured a seat on the Senate Agriculture Committee. My boss Senator Talmadge, the Committee Chairman, created a new subcommittee, the Rural Development Subcommittee, with Humphrey as Chairman. Before Talmadge was chairman of the full committee, I was limited to writing a speech for Talmadge to give on the Senate floor every week about the need for rural development.

Talmadge knew that Humphrey could get more national support for his pet initiative than anyone else could. My job was to staff that subcommittee, and I was allowed to hire additional staff to help me. One of those was John A. Baker, who had been an assistant secretary in the Department of Agriculture in the administration of John F. Kennedy.

We toured the country together to promote our legislation, which would become the Rural Development Act of 1972. As a former Vice President, Humphrey was able to use an Air Force plane for our rural development hearings around the country. We called it Air Force Two. This travel gave me the opportunity to know the man in a way that I would not have otherwise.

No one knew the need for rural development better than Humphrey. He was born in Huron, South Dakota in a room over his father's drugstore before the Great Depression. His father moved first to a larger town in North Dakota, and ultimately to Minneapolis with his drugstore. The young Humphrey was forced to forgo his education for seven years while he worked as a pharmacist in his father's drugstore.

We did fly back out to South Dakota in one of our rural development tours. I still have a memento of that trip. It was in that tour that I remember sitting around the dinner table at night and while Humphrey regaled a group of Republican and Democratic Senators. He was the only senator I have ever known who could do all of the talking and make the other senators love it.

One of our tours was to Georgia, where he spoke to one of the most conservative groups in the State, the Association of County Commissioners. I had some concerns about that, but he soon had them cheering. We then traveled to South Georgia, where we visited a middle school, and he joined a group of children dancing around in a circle. At that same event, two cameramen, one black and one white, got into a shoving match as they jockeyed for position. Humphrey immediately got in the middle and broke it up.

One of the most memorable tours we made was to Alabama. Senator Jim Allen of Alabama was a member of the Committee and insisted we come. I did not think that we should go because Governor George Wallace was a racist and segregationist who had run for President in 1968. He had helped defeat Humphrey when he split the vote in the 1968 race between Richard Nixon and Humphrey. Humphrey lost by less than one percent of the popular vote. Wallace then ran for the presidency one more time and was shot in a campaign rally in Maryland in 1972. This left him paralyzed from his waist down.

Humphrey graciously agreed to come, and we flew to Montgomery, the Capitol city of Alabama. There was Governor Wallace in his wheel chair to meet us and shake hands with Humphrey as he got off the steps from the airplane. Wallace took us to the governor's mansion, where we had a cordial lunch.

Humphrey was a man of great convictions. None but the most extreme leftists could deny he was a liberal. He was primarily responsible for the Senate passage of the Civil Rights Act of 1964. He made another run for the Presidency in 1972, but he lost the nomination to fellow liberal and colleague on the Senate Agriculture Committee, George McGovern.

President Johnson had to step down and not run for reelection because the Vietnam War was so unpopular, and Bobby Kennedy was running against him. The anti-war activists were still mad at Humphrey's service in the Johnson administration, and the more ardent anti-war candidate McGovern captured their imaginations

As Humphrey and McGovern were both members of the Senate Agriculture Committee, I observed they were publicly courteous to each other. I picked up some animosity on Humphrey's part only during a private conversation with him once when both of them were angling to take the lead on legislation to regulate the futures industry (Which would become the Commodity Futures Trading Commission Act of 1974). However Humphrey never let it show in public. He was unfailingly courteous in dealing with his colleagues, whether they were southern segregationists, or antagonists on the left.

For an excellent commentary on Humphrey, see a book written by Ted Van Dyk, "Heroes, Hacks, and Fools". He was a speechwriter and top assistant to Humphrey for the eventful years when Humphrey was Vice President and candidate for the Presidency. When you read it, you are struck with how unfortunate for the country it was that he narrowly lost.

The strongest public indication of displeasure I witnessed from Humphrey was in a committee session where Senator Jesse Helms was speaking. Helms was an extremely conservative North Carolina Republican, but also a gentleman. Humphrey said nothing and simply shook his head in obvious disbelief and disapproval.

Another example of Talmadge and Humphrey collaborating was the National Forest Management Act of 1976. In a court decision the clear cutting was banned in our national forests. It would make the harvesting of timber in our national forests very difficult. More important, it would exacerbate the problem of raging wildfires in our national forests which endangered adjoining residential areas.

Extreme environmentalists such as the Sierra Club opposed cutting trees in our National Forests. To overcome their opposition, I had the bright idea that we should have Humphrey introduce the bill that would serve as the "Chairman's Mark" -- the bill that the committee would use as the markup vehicle. I reasoned that there was no way the environmentalists would attack Humphrey, a liberal icon. I was wrong. Immediately, the Sierra Club issued a press release denouncing Humphrey as a prostitute for the timber industry. I never forgave them for that.

To add to our problems, Scoop Jackson of Washington State chaired the Senate Interior Committee, which had joint Senate jurisdiction over the National Forests. Like Humphrey, he had ambitions to run for President in 1972.

Not to be dismayed, Talmadge chaired a joint markup of the two committees and we promptly went through and reported the bill. Unfortunately, the major timber companies were not entirely happy with the bill, and asked to see Talmadge. He told them to come in to see him the next morning at 7:30 AM. When they came in and sat down, Talmadge said, "Gentlemen, I got you a damn good bill. Don't f--- it up" That was the end of the conversation.

Fortunately, a young congressman named Tom Foley had become chairman of the House Agriculture Committee in 1975. He came from Washington State, where most of the forest lands were in National Forests. With his leadership, companion legislation promptly went through the House and became law, the National Forest Management Act of 1976.

My only regret was that the CEOs of the large timber companies never hired me for any work either when I went into private practice less than two years later or subsequently. They blamed me for the rough way that Talmadge talked to them.

In this bi-partisan time members from both parties learned from each other. There was a moderate young Republican senator from Kansas who came to the Senate after a few terms in the House. His name was Bob Dole.

It was fun to watch Dole and Humphrey banter back and forth across the committee table. It was soon apparent that the young Dole was learning from Humphrey, the old master. After a while, I observed that Dole was taking on some of the habits and tactics of Humphrey, his role model. Like Humphrey, he was destined for greater things. He would go on to become Chairman of the Senate Finance Committee, Majority Leader of the Senate and then run unsuccessfully for Vice President (under Gerald Ford) and for President against Bill Clinton.

The difference between that era and the present is that we got an incredible amount of bipartisan legislation passed in a very short period of time. In my own case, we moved two major legislative initiatives through the Committee and to final enactment almost every year. There was no need for the public to complain about a "do nothing Congress".

In the case of the Senate Agriculture Committee, this was due in large part to Senator Talmadge, who didn't have a partisan bone in his body. He liked some Republicans better than some of his fellow Democrats. Also, he was the man of the fewest words of anyone I have ever known. He was entirely results-oriented. He was only focused on getting the job done ---not on who got the credit.

Today, things move at a snail's pace. An enormous amount of time goes to partisan political posturing and attacks and some important decisions never get made. They just kick the can down the road. Most hard decisions are deferred to future generations.

America's two party system has generally worked well since the days of Thomas Jefferson and John Adams. However, even our founding fathers were more partisan than we like to admit. In Jon Meacham's recent best-selling book, "Thomas Jefferson: The Art of Power", he points out that Jefferson found it necessary to strike compromises with his opposition Federalists in order to effectively govern.

In the depression era of Franklin D. Roosevelt, political rhetoric took a hard left turn toward class warfare, with Roosevelt blasting "the malefactors of great wealth". In the end, FDR's leadership in the Second World War, as well as his aggressive social welfare programs helped our nation overcome both the Great Depression and the socialist sentiments at home. His Agricultural Act of 1938 had to overcome an intransigent Supreme Court. In the 1942 case of Wickard v. Filburn, Roosevelt prevailed, and we have had farm programs ever since.

America's economy eventually recovered, and we assumed a position of world leadership. H. W. Brands did a great job describing FDR in his award-winning biography, "A Traitor to His Class".

When FDR died tragically at the beginning of his fourth term, Harry Truman proved to be an unexpectedly strong President. His plain talk and blunt speech connected with the American people. He campaigned against the "Do-Nothing Congress". The press (and the Gallup Poll) expected Truman to lose to Republican nominee Tom Dewey. In the end Truman won a surprise victory and helped return the country to normalcy. David McCullough did a wonderful job of telling the Truman story in his biography, "Truman". Reading it demonstrates that Truman was a no-nonsense leader who was just interested in getting the job done.

Eisenhower Returns the Country to Normalcy

General Dwight D. Eisenhower was drafted by the Republican Party to run as its candidate in the 1951 Presidential election. He had been courted by the Democratic Party as well, because he was a war hero with no previous political involvement. His Democratic opponent, Adlai Stevenson, was no match for the World War II hero who had led the allies to victory in Europe. Eisenhower was not a compelling speaker, but he was a good administrator who restored calm to a country that was tired of war.

As my friend and mentor Hubert Humphrey wrote in his book, "The Education of a Public Man", the Eisenhower years gave the country a chance for calm and healing. In any event, Eisenhower was a moderate President who was not bound by conservative Republican ideology.

The Kansas born Eisenhower appointed a very conservative Mormon Secretary of Agriculture, Ezra Taft Benson. Farmers had been encouraged to plant fence row to fence row to supply food for the war effort. When our allies in Europe were able to get back to full production, we suddenly had huge surpluses. Persistent farm surpluses and depressed commodity prices forced Eisenhower to take 28 million acres out of production with his soil bank program. Farmers were paid to take their land out of production and put it in pine trees. Had this program begun in a Democratic administration it would have been characterized a liberal supply management program like those of Roosevelt's New Deal.

My first Federal job, as a high school student, was to measure land for acreage allotments and soil bank payments. I observed that most of the acres put in the Soil Bank were planted to pine trees and were harvested for pulpwood. Later, much of the most productive land was cleared and put back into the production of crops. The soil bank program worked exactly as intended.

Eisenhower's greatest peacetime achievement was the construction of the interstate highway system, which was badly needed to bind the nation together and promote development of our vast rural areas. Later, we would build on this through the Talmadge and Humphrey success in passing the Rural Development Act of 1972.

Eisenhower served two full terms. Perhaps the most important thing one can say about Eisenhower was that he brought the nation together. He was not an ideologue. He was a very good healing influence on the nation that had just gone through the agony of a terrible world war.

John F. Kennedy: Promise Cut Short

John Fitzgerald Kennedy was one of the most inspiring and promising Presidents of all time. His inaugural speech line, "Ask not what your country can do for you. Ask what you can do for your can do for your country" is phrase that will stick in my brain forever. He was a handsome young man, and had a very attractive young family. He brought to the race the credentials of a World War II hero and the financial resources of a wealthy father willing to spend whatever it took to get him elected. His wealth enabled him to overwhelm his opponents in the Democratic primaries.

Those opponents included Hubert Humphrey, who never had the financial backing necessary to win against a well-funded candidate such as Kennedy. As Humphrey wrote in his autobiography, he was struggling to travel around the country on old buses, while Kennedy and His team were traveling on jet airplanes. Humphrey had grown up in impoverished circumstances in South Dakota in the Great Depression. He had to defer his education for seven years to help his father survive in the family drugstore.

John Kennedy's 1000 days as President were very eventful. He served during the height of the Cold War and during the communist takeover of Cuba. His most disastrous foreign policy blunder was the botched Bay of Pigs invasion. However, things improved after his facedown of Nikita Khrushchev in the Cuban Missile Crisis.

On the domestic policy front, Kennedy was more fortunate. The economy was growing under Kennedy's initiatives that included a tax cut. People were enchanted by the closest thing to a royal family that we Americans have ever had. Kennedy was very popular, and he would have had no problem in being reelected in 1964. However, his tragic assassination in Dallas on November 22, 1963 cut short his promise. We will never know how he would have handled the Vietnam conflict that brought Lyndon Johnson down. We only know that these events forced Johnson to step down and not run for a second term.

Like millions of other Americans, I can vividly remember exactly where I was and what I was doing when it was announced that President Kennedy had been shot on Nov. 22, 1963. I was standing out in front of the University of Georgia Law School during a morning break. I can even remember the crude remark by right-wing redneck guy who said "I hope whoever shot him was a good shot so he hit his little brain".

Only a few months later, I had moved to Washington and joined the Capitol Police Force so I could work my way through law school. I was on the day shift before I could get into law school. My most memorable experience occurred when I stood Guard in the Capitol Rotunda as General Douglas MacArthur lay in state in an open casket in April 1964. Many of the rich and famous from all over the world filed by to pay their respects.

Little did I know that later I would come to counsel JA Zenchu, which represents the farmers of Japan. This prompted me to read "American Caesar: Douglas MacArthur 1880 - 1964" by William Manchester.

Lyndon Baines Johnson

Lyndon Johnson was never a popular national politician. He became President only when John F. Kennedy was assassinated. To most Americans, Johnson was an unknown quantity. He was not a naturally likable or eloquent politician. Where Kennedy was handsome, stylish and eloquent, Johnson was often coarse and crude. Where Kennedy had grown up as a child of great privilege, Johnson grew up desperately poor in the hill country of East Texas. An adequate analysis of such a controversial character is not possible in a book like this. This book is written to demonstrate how and why people have come to distrust their elected officials and why so often our Federal government is in political gridlock.

Distinguished author Robert Caro has made a notable career of writing about Lyndon Johnson. He has written a series of books that are available on Amazon, either in print or on Kindle. Johnson's years growing up as a driven young underprivileged boy in the years of the Great Depression and his path to the House are chronicled in Caro's "Path to Power".

In Caro's "Means of Ascent" he takes Johnson through his service as a young congressman in World War II and the foundation of his long-secret fortune, as well as the facts behind the myths he created about it. One of the most interesting features of the book is Caro's revelation of the true story of the fiercely contested 1948 senatorial election. This was the race that Johnson had to win or face political extinction. He did win it--by "the 87 votes that changed history." They called him "Landslide Lyndon". This is good account of a huge turning point in American politics. It was the last stand of the old politics and the beginning of the new -- the old politics of issues versus the new politics of image, mass manipulation, money and demonization of one's opponent.

Johnson's years as Vice President and his taking over the powers of the Presidency are described in the "Passage of Power". Also, Caro's report on the events surrounding the Kennedy assassination is described in his short book "Dallas". These books leave readers with the belief that Johnson was an unsavory character, both in building his fortune and in manipulating his way to the Presidency.

Johnson had an unquenchable thirst for money, power and sex. He kept several affairs going at all times. He was reported to have said, "I got more by accident than Kennedy got on purpose". People felt sorry for his shy, unglamorous wife, Lady Byrd. When Johnson was climbing to power, she served him breakfast in bed every morning, and she would entertain his cronies with huge meals prepared at short notice

He was widely reported to have had affairs with several women who worked in his office. When I worked on the midnight shift of the Capitol Police Force, the old timers would tell stories of Johnson coming out of one of his Capitol hideaways after midnight with a beautiful young woman. He accumulated offices all over the Capitol when he was Majority Leader, and kept all of them when he was Vice-President.

However, astute observers say that Lady Byrd was much more important to Johnson that people thought. She was the one Johnson confided in during his periods of deep depression and physical illnesses. She was also essential to his early rise in Texas, as she came from money, while he was desperately poor. It is clear that without Lady Byrd, he could never have risen to power.

I never had the chance to know Johnson. However, I did get to know one of his best friends in the Senate. I became acquainted with former Senator George Smathers when he was lobbying me for the Chicago Board of Trade on the legislation to establish the Commodity

Futures Trading Commission. He had been the best Senate friend of John Kennedy, and had participated in the wedding of JFK and Jaqueline Bouvier. Both Kennedy and Smathers were handsome, dapper young Senators with an eye for the ladies.

When Smathers and his young associate Tad Davis would take me to lunch, Smathers would say, "I think I will just walk along behind and look at the pretty ladies". Of course, Smathers had no interest in the technical process of drafting legislation to regulate the futures industry. Carl Rose and I would stay late at night and draft the legislation. Tad would come by at night and see how we were doing.

Smathers told me why he retired from the Senate. He was Secretary of the Democratic Caucus when Lyndon Johnson was the Majority Leader. He said Johnson was hard to keep up with. He would work all day and then they would make the rounds for half the night. He said Johnson was working him to death, and it looked like Johnson and Maggie (Warren Magnuson, Chairman of the powerful Senate Commerce Committee) would be in the Senate forever. Therefore, he retired, and became a very successful lobbyist.

Tad Davis was a young tax lawyer who worked for Smathers. He soon became dissatisfied with what Smathers was paying him. Later, he talked to me, and we decided to form the firm of Davis & McLeod at 499 South Capitol Street S.W. The Chicago Board of Trade was our main client.

From numerous sources, it seems clear that Kennedy was planning to dump Johnson for his second term and get a moderate southern governor like Terry Sanford of North Carolina to serve as his running mate.

Caro has committed to a fifth volume to complete his five volume series. One can only speculate whether it will deal definitively with the Kennedy assassination. The single bullet conclusion of the Warren Commission has been thoroughly debunked. Several books on this subject have been written and are available on Amazon.

After Kennedy's assassination, President Johnson faced unforeseen difficulties. First, US direct involvement in the unpopular War in Vietnam was growing. Also, he had to deal with racial unrest at home. He also had less than a year until the 1964 Presidential Election.

Fortunately for Johnson, he had an easy opponent to defeat. Barry Goldwater was both a principled and very likable Senator from Arizona. However, his extreme conservatism made him an easy target. His most famous quote was, "I would remind you that extremism in the defense of liberty is no vice. And let me remind you also that moderation in the pursuit of justice is no virtue". His 1960 book, "The Conscience of a Conservative" was a well written exposition on his conservative philosophy.

Goldwater had the habit of making hawkish statements about the communists that gave rise to concerns that he could lead us into a nuclear war. Johnson's campaign team was able to use Goldwater's trigger-happy words against him. Most damaging to Goldwater was one campaign TV ad.

This ad showed a little girl in a field, counting as she plucked the petals from a daisy. As she counted, a male voice, deep and ominous, counted backward from 10, getting progressively louder. The male voice reached zero as the girl reached 10, and the scene was rent by a nuclear explosion. As a mushroom cloud rose, a tape of Johnson's voice said: "These are the stakes, to make a world in which all of God's children can live or go into the dark. We must either love each other, or we must die."

This advertisement is perhaps the most famous in campaign history. It set the stage for modern day negative campaign ads. After this ad and some of his own statements that were used against him, Goldwater never had a chance. He carried only six states and 36 percent of the popular vote in 1964.

Unlike Johnson had done, Goldwater chose not to try and run simultaneously for President and for reelection in the Senate, he was out of public office for four years. However, he came back and ran successfully for 3 more terms in the Senate. That was when I had the chance to observe him in the Senate. He was a distinguished looking old Senator who got along well with the two Senators I worked for, Talmadge and Humphrey. He was regarded as an American original.

Lyndon Johnson's tenure as President began with a burst of energy. He worked feverishly to pass new social legislation. The New Frontier of John Kennedy became the Great Society program of Johnson. Because he had been an expert at how to pass legislation in both the House and Senate, he was able to enact a record amount of new legislation. Also, he retained as much of the staff of Kennedy as possible.

Johnson's increasing problems in Vietnam made his domestic social programs harder to pay for. He had to try to appease his fiscally conservative friends in the Senate, like Senator Richard B Russell, the old Georgia Senator who was the most respected member of the Senate. Johnson courted Russell, a life-long bachelor, assiduously. He had Russell down to dine in the White House frequently. He taught his two daughters to call him "Uncle Dick".

I remember that for Johnson's 1968 fiscal year budget he had to repeatedly juggle the numbers until the entire federal budget came in slightly under $100 billion. It came in at $99.7 billion. Those were the days before we had House and Senate Budget Committees.

Unfortunately, the morass of the War in Vietnam only became worse. With the passage of the Tonkin Gulf Resolution Johnson put his personal stamp on the war. It went from being only the war in Vietnam to the war in Vietnam, Laos, and Cambodia. This would enable Bobby Kennedy to mount a campaign in the Democratic Primary against him. It appears certain that Bobby Kennedy would have defeated him.

Unfortunately, Kennedy's run was abruptly ended by his assassination on June 5, 1968 in Los Angeles by a lone gunman named Sirhan Sirhan. This was unlike the case of his brother Jack's assassination in 1963, where JFK's assassin Lee Harvey Oswald, was immediately assassinated by Jack Ruby. In the case of Bobby Kennedy, there is no indication that there was a conspiracy. His killer is still alive in prison, and would have repeatedly had the chance to implicate other members of a conspiracy.

Sirhan is a Palestinian of Jordanian citizenship and is currently serving a life sentence at the Richard J. Donovan Correctional Facility in San Diego County, California. He was born in British-ruled Jerusalem and hated Israel. In 1989, he told David Frost, "My only connection with Robert Kennedy was his sole support of Israel and his deliberate attempt to send those 50 bombers to Israel to obviously do harm to the Palestinians."

This assassination was the first major incident of political violence in the United States stemming from the Arab–Israeli conflict in the Middle East. This was decades before the 9-11 take down of the Twin Towers in New York City and the continuing war against terrorism.

The assassination of Bobby Kennedy removed Johnson's major political opponent, but he had already announced his intention to step down on March 31. The casualties in Vietnam continued to mount, and Johnson could not reverse his earlier decision not to run again.

Vice President Humphrey was loyal to President Johnson, and did not want him to step down. However, within days Humphrey had privately decided to run for the Presidency of the United States. As Humphrey recounted in his biography "The Education of a Public Man", he faced many obstacles. The greatest of these was his close association with President Johnson and the War in Vietnam.

The Humphrey campaign was stalled for a month after the assassination of Bobby Kennedy. Everyone was depressed. When Humphrey did get his campaign fully in gear, he had only a few months until Election Day. Also, the Democratic Convention was set for Chicago on August 27, Johnson's birthday. Humphrey tried in vain to get Johnson (still the titular leader of the Democratic Party) to agree to change both the date and the place, but Johnson refused.

This was only one of the cases when Johnson's stubbornness undermined Humphrey's chances of being elected. Another was his manic opposition to Humphrey coming out with any position on Vietnam that was inconsistent with his own. This is one case where Humphrey's great human decency proved fatal.

 When Humphrey finally did break with the Johnson policy, the momentum of the campaign immediately changed. He got the support of young people who had opposed him. He narrowly lost to Nixon. In his autobiography, he wrote that he realized he made a mistake in waiting that long to make the break from Johnson. This is just another case of Humphrey's great humanity. His loyalty deprived him of the ultimate prize, the Presidency of the United States. He lost in the popular vote by less than one percentage of the popular vote-- Richard Nixon 43.4%, Hubert Humphrey 42.7%, George Wallace 13.5%.

After analyzing Johnson's career, I concluded he was one our most conflicted Presidents ever. He wanted to bring the country together in his "Great Society", but he was obsessed with winning the impossible war in Vietnam. This left the country badly divided.

The Long Nixon Nightmare

Richard Nixon was the 37th U.S. President and the only commander-in-chief forced to resign from his position. He was brought down by the Watergate scandal. His fall was one of the most traumatic periods in American history. It left scars in our nation that will never go away.

Like many other figures in the history of America, Nixon grew up in very harsh circumstances. However, he overcame tremendous obstacles and political defeats to rise to the Presidency of the United States, making him the most important man in the world.

Nixon changed the political system of the United States forever. His name became synonymous with the Washington corruption in the "Watergate" scandal. Watergate was only the name of a hotel, condominium, and office building development in Washington D.C. It was the location of the Democratic National Committee (DNC). Nixon's efforts to break in and spy on the DNC were the scandal that brought him down.

Watergate was the event that triggered the elevation of Congressman Gerald Ford to the Presidency as well as Ford's defeat three years later by an obscure Georgia governor, Jimmy Carter. A majority of voters could not forgive Ford's pardon of Nixon.

Watergate had quite an effect on me in my formative years. As an idealistic young man who had just recently started work in the Senate, I was sickened as the Watergate scandal unfolded. I remember being at a rural development hearing in Atlanta with Talmadge and Humphrey when Talmadge mused that it would be unbelievable if the Attorney General John Mitchell were involved.

A special investigating committee was empaneled in the Senate. The public hearings were conducted in the historic Senate Caucus Room adjacent to the Senate Agriculture Committee, where I worked. In fact, our offices there were used as a holding room where witnesses and their lawyers sat while waiting their turn. Since my boss, Senator Talmadge was busy as one of the seven members of the Watergate Committee; we were not having any hearings of our own. I would often watch these hearings next door, a little resentful that we were not doing more in the Agriculture Committee.

There were a number of bright young men who got involved in the Watergate Debacle. One

who sat in our offices with his attorney was Jeb
Stuart Magruder. I remember thinking "there is
no way that such a nice looking young man
could be involved in an illegal break-in". In
Magruder's case, he did serve prison time, but
this forced him to reevaluate his life. He
returned to his religious roots and earned a
Masters of Divinity from Princeton. He became
a Presbyterian minister, and has written some
books about his life experiences.

A young lawyer friend of mine, Bob
McCandless from Oklahoma, served as
counsel to his brother in law, John Dean,
another young lawyer. Dean was culpable
because he was in charge of the Watergate
cover-up. Dean had served as Counsel to
President Nixon. When things began to close in
on Nixon, Dean was supposed to serve as the
fall guy. That is why he turned state's evidence
against Nixon.

Dean did not escape some time in jail. He
pleaded guilty to a single felony count in
exchange for becoming a key witness for the
prosecution. This ultimately resulted in a
reduced prison sentence, which he served at
Fort Holabird outside Baltimore, Maryland.

The involvement of Dean in Watergate
destroyed his legal career. However, he has

written several books, and he brought down the career of Earl Butz, who I knew as Secretary of Agriculture under Presidents Nixon and Ford.

Dean was on a commercial flight returning from the 1976 Republican Convention. In a conversation with Pat Boone, Butz told an unusually offensive joke about blacks. Dean had been to the convention to report for Rolling Stone Magazine. Butz loved to tell dirty jokes to anyone he met. Rolling Stone published this joke in every vulgar detail. There was public outrage, and Butz was promptly forced to resign.

G Gordon Liddy was a case so bizarre that it could not be made up by a fiction writer. He was a lawyer who had many posts, including a member of the FBI, and running unsuccessfully for public office. As for Watergate, he was counsel to the committee to reelect the president (CREP). He job was to bug the offices of the Democratic National Committee (DNC). He did not get caught in the DNC, but he directed the operation from an adjoining suite in the Watergate Hotel.

Without going into the details, which are readily available on Wikipedia and other web sites, Liddy was one of the first casualties when the Watergate scandal began to unravel. He ultimately served four and a half years in prison, more than any other Watergate criminal.

What is most interesting to me is that he has become the most publicly and financially successful of all those brought down by the Watergate scandal. He wrote a book about his Watergate experiences " Will: The Autobiography of G. Gordon Liddy". He has starred in Television shows and on talk shows.

Liddy, is still around. The last I saw of him was that he was pitching gold on television for the company Rosland Capital. I guess that just proves that anything is possible in America.

The hearings of the Watergate Committee, more formally known as the Senate Select Committee on Presidential Campaign Activities, were historic by any standard. They were nationally televised, so they were much in the consciousness of the American people. They laid out the evidence that demonstrated Nixon's guilt in the Watergate break-in and other dirty tricks. Nixon never was convicted or went to jail. However, 40 of his aides did.

The most important of those was John Mitchell, the Attorney General. He was convicted of conspiracy, obstruction of justice, and perjury in the break-in of the Watergate offices of Larry

O'Brien and the subsequent cover-up. He was sentenced to two and a half to eight years in the federal prison at Maxwell Air Force Base in Montgomery Alabama. However, he was allowed out for medical reasons after serving 19 months.

One of my vivid memories was the morning when I was coming into the entrance to the Russell Senate Office Building, where I worked. As I walked in, Chuck Colson ran by me on his way out. He was clearly quite flustered and upset. Later, I read that Colson, Special Counsel to the President, had gone to ask for help from Senator Weickert, a maverick Republican member of the Watergate Committee. Weickert was so enraged that he took his Yale paddle to Colson and threw him out of his office.

Colson was the first member of the Nixon staff to serve time in prison because of his involvement in the Watergate scandal and role as Nixon's hatchet man. He served 7 months in federal prison in Montgomery, Alabama. However, he had a mid-life conversion to Christianity and founded the Prison Fellowship, his group to minister to those in prisons. He also authored 30 books.

The hearings also had the effect of making the career of some young people. The two young Washington Post reporters, Bob Woodward and Carl Bernstein, did yeoman work when they were assigned to work on the routine burglary of the Democratic National Committee offices at the Watergate. In addition to books Woodward has written about Watergate, he went on to write several other terrific books about subsequent presidents and wars.

Another rookie reporter who became famous was Lesley Stahl. She had the good fortune to cover the Watergate hearings for CBS. I remember seeing her when she came to a pool side party of Senator Talmadge and his wife Betty. Stahl went on to become White House correspondent during the presidencies of Jimmy Carter, Ronald Reagan and George H. W. Bush. Today, Stahl remains a mainstay of the CBS program "60 Minutes", the longest running and most successful Sunday evening news program.

Senator Sam Ervin of North Carolina was appointed Chairman of the Watergate Committee. At the time he was a little known senator from North Carolina who was a Constitutional scholar and former jurist from North Carolina. Though he was Harvard trained, he described himself as "just a country lawyer". The televised Watergate hearings made him a folk hero. He later wrote some books and was the subject of biographies.

The ranking Republican and Vice Chairman of the Committee, Howard Baker, was a moderate young senator from Tennessee whose career was boosted by these hearings. He was the son-in-law of Senator Everett Dirksen, long-time Republican leader of the Senate. He later became Senate Majority Leader and even attempted his own bid for the Presidency in 1980.

Baker's performance on the Watergate Committee was the most impressive because he started out the process on Nixon's side. Nixon had worked to help Baker get elected to his first term in the Senate in a period when Nixon was out of office. Republicans were confident that the boyish- looking southerner and trial lawyer would defend the White House. His 1972 campaign literature described him as a "close friend and trusted advisor of our President, Richard M. Nixon."

Baker framed the central question of the hearings, "What did the President know, and when did he know it?" It surprised most people that he was actually interested in finding out the truth rather than protecting a fellow Republican.

However, he and other members of the Watergate Committee, both Democrats and Republicans, did pursue the facts wherever they led. My boss Talmadge, a former trial lawyer, certainly did.

Baker's chief counsel on the committee was a bright young Tennessee trial lawyer named Fred Thompson. He sat right beside Baker in the lengthy nationally televised hearings, so he had a lot of face time on national television. He was the one who was allowed to ask Alexander Butterfield the pivotal question that revealed the secret taping system in the Oval Office. Without these tapes, Nixon would have never gone down.

The recognition that Thompson received enabled him to get elected to the Senate in his own right. He served for 8 years before resigning to become a successful feature film and television actor. He even tried unsuccessfully to mount a bid for the Presidency in 2008. He was most recently seen on television doing commercials for reverse mortgages, which try to lure old people to take out the equity in their homes to live on until they die. Unfortunately, Thompson died at age 73 from Lymphoma.

Later, I was a partner of retired Senator Hugh Scott in the law firm Scott, Harrison & McLeod. Senator Scott had been the moderate Senate Republican Leader during the Watergate scandal. It was he who told Richard Nixon that Senate Republicans would not support him if the House impeached him. If the House impeached, he would be convicted. Thus, Nixon was forced to resign in order to avoid the impeachment and conviction process.

This entire episode was bizarre. Nixon did not need to do anything illegal to get reelected. In his 1972 reelection, he wound up scoring one of the most lop-sided victories in the annals of presidential elections. His opponent, George McGovern, won the electoral votes of only Massachusetts and the District of Columbia.

On a personal level, McGovern was as nice a gentleman as you could ever meet. He was not the wild-eyed liberal he had been painted to be. However, he never had a chance of defeating Nixon.

After, the Senate ethics nightmare that Talmadge went through, McGovern understood the personal toll it took on me. He called me into his Senate office to ask me to help with his reelection campaign for his Senate seat in South Dakota. I was flattered and tried to help him get elected to another term in the Senate, but to no avail. He state had turned too red, and he was defeated in 1980, the same year that Talmadge was defeated for reelection in Georgia. Today, a Democrat would never have a chance of being elected in South Dakota.

I never understood the paranoia of Nixon. As an idealistic young man, I had trouble coming to grips with it for a long time. I could not bear to read the book "The Final Days" by Woodward and Bernstein or view the movie based on if. I just wanted to forget this horrible blemish on our democracy.

In my research for this book, I read the subsequent books by Bob Woodward. "The Last of the President's Men" is the best I have read on Nixon. It is about the role of Alexander Butterfield, the able young Air Force officer who served as Nixon's Deputy Chief of Staff. It was his disclosure of Nixon's secret taping system that ultimately brought Nixon down.

Butterfield made his unpublished memoirs and his boxes of files available to Woodward. He submitted to hours of video taping by Woodward. He did all of this for no compensation whatever. For those who are interested in American history, I strongly recommend this book.

Perhaps, the book's most revealing insight into how weird Nixon was is the revelation that he would communicate with his wife Patricia through memos where he would refer to himself in the third person. The memos would say "To Mrs. Nixon from the President" and would be signed "RN". Butterfield concluded she was a borderline abused wife.

One of the many unfortunate things about Watergate is that It cast a shadow over the five succeeding Presidents--Ford, Carter, Reagan, Bush, and Clinton. Bob Woodward described this very well in his 1999 book, "Shadow, Five Presidents and the Legacy of Watergate".

In fact Woodward understated this shadow. It had the same chilling effect on Congress and the people who deal with it. No longer can you even buy a congressman lunch. The only legally proper way to do it is through attending a PAC luncheon. This also applies to lunches with congressional staff.

Gerald Ford ended the Long National Nightmare

After Nixon resigned, Gerald Ford, the Vice President, was immediately sworn in as President. He was one of the most thoroughly decent and honorable men to ever occupy the White House. His wife Betty was an ideal partner as his First Lady. Her notable personal achievement was to found the Betty Ford Center for treatment of alcoholism and other addictions in 1982.

Ford's sincerity was sometimes misinterpreted as him being simple-minded. Moreover, a stumble he made while getting off a plane on a foreign trip convinced many people he was a klutz. Both impressions were erroneous. He was an outstanding football player at the University of Michigan, where he led the team to two undefeated seasons and two national championships. He also won an award as the most valuable player. Later, he would graduate from Yale Law School in the top 25% of his class.

Ford had been appointed President under the 25th Amendment of the Constitution. It was an unusual sequence of events, because Vice-President Agnew was forced to resign to avoid prosecution for taking bribes while he had served as governor of Maryland. On October,

13, 1973, following Spiro Agnew's resignation two days earlier, President Richard Nixon nominated Representative Gerald Ford of Michigan to succeed Agnew as Vice President. On August 9, 1974, Richard Nixon resigned and Gerald Ford was immediately sworn in as the 38th President of the United States.

Ford correctly saw that it was his duty to heal the nation after the trauma of the Nixon Impeachment. After some consideration, he decided to pardon Nixon. In his national address on Sept. 8, 1974, he said "Our long national nightmare is over". However, many voters resented the fact that he had pardoned Nixon. That did more than anything to result in his defeat by an obscure southern governor during his bid for reelection in 1976. It did not help that America's economy suffered its worst recessions since the Great Depression three decades ago.

Ford became the first sitting president to debate his challenger. Ford appeared to win the first debate, but made a bad blunder in the second, thus allowing his critics to say he wasn't very bright. Even with that, Ford almost pulled it off. His opponent, Jimmy Carter, committed a serious blunder with a Playboy interview in which he said he had lust in his heart for women other than his wife. Most married men know that you never admit that to your wife, and certainly not to Playboy.

Jimmy Carter: The Accidental President

As a young Senate staffer who was doing the agricultural policy work for Carter's campaign, I was scared to death. In the end, Carter won with only 50.1% of the popular vote. If Ford had won only the two swing states of Ohio and Wisconsin next to his Michigan home state, he would have been victorious. Carter became the first President elected from the Deep South since Zachary Taylor in 1848, before the Civil War.

Surprisingly, this election set a great example of how victorious Presidents should treat their predecessors. Carter and his wife Rosalyn went out of their way to invite the Fords to the White House to dine with them when the Fords came back to Washington. Also they would visit the Fords when President Carter traveled to Michigan.

Unfortunately, this kind of courtesy has not been extended to the Carters since they left the White House--either by Republican or Democratic Presidents.

There has never been a President who was a better man and more devout Christian than Carter. Of course, I was a fellow South Georgian who grew up about a two hours' drive from his home in Plains, so I am probably biased. However, I am absolutely sure that no one tried harder than he to heal the divisions in our country. He is in no way responsible for the political divisions that often paralyze our government today. He was elected because of public revulsion at the corruption and paranoia of Richard Nixon.

Pat Caddell, Carter's pollster, subsequently said in an interview, "Going from total anonymity, to being President of the United States in less than twelve months is unprecedented in American history. If it weren't for the country looking for something in '76, Carter could never have gotten elected". Carter's pledge to the American people was very simple, "You can trust me, I will never lie to you".

No President, before or since, has been able to get elected on that simple platform. However, the only qualification of some who are competing for the Republican nomination in 2016 is that they are Washington outsiders. Some have never held any elective office.

I remember flying with chicken magnate Don Tyson to a campaign meeting in Iowa with Carter when he was mounting his first Presidential campaign. When he spoke to the voters, Carter exhibited a marvelous mastery of the details of all issues, but his pledge to never lie to the voters was what propelled him to victory in the Iowa caucus and to victory in the Democratic primary.

He had promised a new beginning. He said he would heal the wounds of Watergate and Vietnam. He would give us a government "as good and decent and compassionate as the American people." But events would soon overwhelm him. He had to deal with an energy crisis that produced long lines at gas stations, and inflation was rampant.

One of Carter's problems as a Washington outsider was that he brought in key staff with no more Washington experience than he. One example of this was his choice of the leader of his transition team. This is a vitally important job for a new president. He must be prepared to get his team in place as soon as he is sworn in.

To head his transition team, Carter picked a bright young Atlanta lawyer, Jack Watson. He was a Phi Beta Kappa graduate of Vanderbilt University who received his law degree from Harvard Law School. He served in the U.S. in the Marine Corps and left with the rank of Captain. Unfortunately, Watson had no experience in Washington politics. He did not know to be careful about hiring people who had their own personal agenda which might be quite different than that of President.

One such case was Carter's appointment of an extreme consumer activist, Carol Tucker Forman from Arkansas, to serve as the Assistant Secretary of Agriculture. Her responsibility included poultry and meat inspection. She was well connected in Arkansas as the sister of Jim Guy Tucker, who succeeded Bill Clinton as governor of Arkansas. Since I had been close to the Carter campaign, both she and Mike Pertchuk had sought my support for positions in the new Carter administration. She received her appointment, and Pertchuk was appointed Chairman of the Federal Trade Commission.

Pertchuk turned out to be the nemesis of the business community, as he aggressively pursued his own personal agenda. He fancied himself the ultimate consumer advocate and greatly expanded the Anti-Trust jurisdiction of the FTC. In. the business community, he became the Carter Administration's most hated regulator. I will never believe this was Carter's agenda. It was only that of Pertchuk.

The Department of Agriculture nominees had to go through the Senate Agriculture Committee, and I helped Chairman Talmadge get my friend Bob Bergland confirmed in record time. I tried to do the same thing for Forman. The committee's ranking Republican Bob Dole objected to her. I talked to some of the interest groups to bring pressure on him. Dole had to yield, but he had hard feelings against me for the rest of my time as Staff Director. He would refer to me in the press as "the partisan staff director".

However, he has been quite gracious to me since I went into private practice. He publicly praised me at a memorial service for Martin Sorkin, the long-time Washington lobbyist for Dole's old friend Dwayne Andreas. He is the same guy who was Hubert Humphrey's first financial backer for election as Mayor of Minneapolis.

Carol Tucker Forman described chicken processing as washing chickens in a fecal bath. She also maintained that eggs were bad for your health because of their high level of cholesterol, an accusation that would be later thoroughly debunked by science. It was later proven that there was no relationship between dietary cholesterol and blood cholesterol in humans. I arranged a little summit meeting that included her titular boss, Secretary of Agriculture Bob Bergland, Chairman Talmadge and I, and we got her to back off. Tyson and the rest of the chicken and egg industry had to rely on those of us on the Senate Agriculture Committee to protect them from this extremism.

In the election of 1980, Carter, the former peanut farmer from Georgia, could not even get the votes of farmers. Later I got to know Dick Lyng, who was Ronald Reagan's farm campaign manager. He said, "All I had to do was tell farmers that Carter planned to make Carol Tucker Foreman the next Secretary of Agriculture".

Another thing that hurt Carter among farmers was a sharp economic downturn that created unprecedented farmer unrest. The American Agriculture Movement staged a national revolt and drove their tractors into Washington. They parked them on the Washington Mall. They occupied the buildings of the US Department of Agriculture and made the life of my old friend Secretary Bergland miserable. They tramped up and down the hallways of the Capitol buildings. I had hired a blunt speaking economist on the committee staff. Because he told the demonstrators the truth, they tried to beat him up. I had to tell him not to come into the office for a while.

Carter had come to Washington with good intentions, but no experience in dealing with national issues or working with Congress. Worse yet, his top staff had no experience. Democratic House Speaker Tip O'Neal would refer to his chief of staff, Hamilton Jordan, as "Hannibal Jerkin". Dan Tate, who had come to work under me as a legislative assistant to Senator Talmadge did go over to the White House as Carter's congressional lobbyist. He did a good job of helping Carter in this area.

One of Carter's failings was that he was obsessed with details. He would keep on his desk the schedule of the White House tennis court, and he would determine who could use it. When his cabinet met on farm policy, he could describe in detail how the obscure oat program worked.

.

Despite his handicaps in learning Washington ways, President Carter, the ultimate workaholic, did achieve a lot. In foreign relations, he negotiated the Panama Canal Treaty and got it ratified by two thirds of the Senate. He worked tirelessly for peace in the Middle East. In domestic affairs, he deregulated the airlines and led the deregulation of the trucking industry. He was a reformer, and attempted to restrain government spending by implementing "zero based budgeting". This was the budgeting process he had implemented while Governor of Georgia.

The focus of Carter's foreign policy was human rights, which conformed to his Christian world view. He was concerned about our support for many dictatorships where human rights were disregarded. It the case of Iran he failed to support an old ally, the Shah of Iran. The Shah had been returned to power in Iran by the British and American governments in 1953.

I did not agree with Carter's opinion of the Shah because I had a good friend in Reinhardt Junior College who worshipped the Shah. Irag Moustoufi was the son of a prosperous textile merchant in Iran. He attended this little college to better learn English. Since he had read more of America's great books than I had, I was quite impressed by him. He referred to his nation as Persia, not Iran. He pointed out that his culture was much greater than mine because mine was only two hundred years old while his was thousands of years old.

 Once I told Moustoufi that I admired a shirt he was wearing. He insisted on trying to give it to me. That is the only time that anyone has tried to give me the shirt on his back

Later my dentist and prosthodontist would be a young Iranian man who reminded me of my friend in Reinhardt College.

President Carter's desertion of the Shah, enabled radical Islam, led by the cleric Ayotolla Khomeini, take over the government of Iran. Khomeini had been exiled in England during the reign of the Shah. This was the first time that radical Islam was to run a modern caliphate. Ultimately, it would doom Carter's chances of being reelected. It did so in two ways.

First, it created shortages of oil and resulted in long lines at the gas pumps. Second, it was a huge national embarrassment when this radical cleric took over and immediately arrested the 53 Americans that were in the country. They were held hostage for 444 days. What happened to our hostages was chronicled by the 2012 movie "Argo", directed by Ben Affleck.

The embarrassment got worse when Carter sent in a team to rescue the captives. It failed. Eight American soldiers were killed, and five were injured.

These 53 hostages were finally released after Carter was defeated in the polls. They were then released during the Reagan inaugural.

Carter was present at the inaugural ceremony at the front of the Capitol as Air Force planes returning the hostages flew overhead during Reagan's inaugural ceremony.

The national humiliation by the Iranian Militants did more than anything to defeat Carter in his bid for reelection. Carter had defeated Ted Kennedy in the Democratic primary. He also lost some votes to independent John Anderson. Ironically, Iran continues to be the greatest threat to world peace today.

Carter is the gold standard for how former Presidents should conduct themselves. Unlike some recent former Presidents, he has not tried to enrich himself with huge speaking fees. His public service continued after his Presidency. On behalf of his Carter Center, he has traveled the world monitoring elections and fighting poverty. He helped found a charity for building homes for the poor in this country, Habitat for Humanity. He still teaches Sunday school every Sunday in the little Baptist church in his home town of Plains, Georgia. With all of that, he has managed to write a new book just about every year.

Recently, Carter has had to fight a new challenge. He was diagnosed with cancer of the liver and the brain. Rather than issue a statement through a spokesman, he spoke directly to the press. He was surprisingly calm and upbeat in making his remarks. Fortunately he appears to have recovered. As this is written, he has been declared cancer-free by his doctors.

Carter noted at the news conference that get-well wishes have poured in from President Obama and all living former presidents, as well as from Secretary of State John F. Kerry and former Secretary of State Hillary Rodham Clinton. "It's the first time they've called me in a long time," Carter joked.

It is too bad that former Presidents and leaders in his own party have not sought Carter's counsel. He would have been honest enough to help his successors avoid his own mistakes. In the last two years of his life, Hubert Humphrey tried to do this for Carter. I know from talking to his chief of staff Hamilton Jordan that Carter valued Humphrey's advice.

Carter is the second-oldest living president, separated by just over 100 days in age from George H.W. Bush. He served in the White House from 1977 to 1981. After his presidency, he continued his humanitarian and human rights work through the Carter Center. He was awarded a Nobel Peace Prize for that.

Ronald Reagan: Morning in America

When Ronald Reagan came to Washington as President, I had a lot of doubts about him. He had soundly defeated Jimmy Carter, in whose campaigns I had worked in 1976 and in 1980. Carter is the only President who had offered me a job in his administration. I had declined an opportunity to go to work in the Carter administration as the chairman of that new little agency we gave birth to in the Senate Agriculture Committee in 1974, the Commodity Futures Trading Commission.

I had remained loyal to Carter and worked hard to get him reelected. So did the chicken magnate Don Tyson of Tyson's Foods, who flew around his farm campaign team in his private jet. It is hard to believe that Tyson still supported Carter after the way Forman treated his business. After Carter was defeated, Tyson showed his class by inviting those of us who were on his agricultural team to be his guest on his fishing boat at Bimini. Only two of us went, and I was upset that more did not avail themselves of his hospitality.

I was certainly glad Carter did not appoint me to be the one job I wanted, Deputy Secretary of Agriculture. The ingratitude of these farmers made me realize that I should not stay much longer in my position of Staff Director of the Senate Agriculture Committee.

One of my proudest achievements had been my role in helping Bob Bergland, Minnesota protégé of Hubert Humphrey, get appointed Secretary of Agriculture. He was a friend while he was in Congress, and I had the privilege of calling him from the 1976 Democratic Convention in New York to see if he was interested in being Secretary. He was out on his farm hauling gravel, but he called back to say he was interested.

The Most Important Thing I Ever Did.

In some other appointments, Carter did not show good judgement as well. He did offer me the job of chairing the new little agency we had created, the Commodity Futures Trading Commission. I had heavy family obligations because my first wife was an invalid; I needed to go into the private sector to earn some money.

Then, he appointed for the Chairman position a young Harvard PH.D. Economist named James Stone. His qualifications were 1) writing a book titled "One Way for Wall Street" and 2) marrying the widow of Supreme Court Justice William O. Douglas. He soon had a nervous breakdown, and had to take leave from his government duties to get psychiatric help.

By contrast, when Reagan was elected he appointed my old friend Phil Johnson to chair the CFTC. Johnson had been the outside counsel to the Chicago Board of Trade when Carl Rose and I were drafting the law which created the CFTC. We did not have the expertise to draft the statute to regulate the futures industry.

Therefore, we traveled to Chicago to learn. However the traders resented us. The said "how can you, who know nothing about our business draft a law to regulate us? Thus we spent time with the young economist of the Chicago Board of Trade (CBOT) Richard Sandor. He spent all the time we needed and took us to dinner. With his help and the legal guidance of Phillip Johnson, we drafted the Commodity Futures Trading Commission Act of 1974.

When Johnson was appointed by Reagan to chair the CFTC, he served with distinction and negotiated the Shad-Johnson Accord with the Chairman of the SEC. This was badly needed to resolve jurisdictional differences between the two top federal agencies charged with the regulation of our financial markets by trading off-exchange. It has stood the test of time until too many transactions escaped regulation. We could see this coming, but Wall Street had more clout than Chicago. When I represented the Chicago Board of Trade, its President Tom Donovan had several staff meetings to discuss what we could do about it.

When Johnson was appointed by President Reagan to chair the CFTC, he served with distinction and negotiated the Shad-Johnson Accord with the Chairman of the SEC. This was badly needed to resolve jurisdictional differences between the two top federal agencies charged with the regulation of our financial markets.

This agreement stood the test of time—until too many transactions escaped regulation. We could see this coming, but Wall Street had more clout than Chicago. When I represented the Chicago Board of Trade, its president, Tom Donovan, had several staff meetings to discuss what we could do about it.

Unfortunately, Senate Banking Committee Chairman Phil Gramm pushed through the Gramm-Leach-Bliley Act, known as the Financial Services Act of 1999. These changes in law were responsible for the Great Recession of 2008, the worst financial crisis since the Great Depression. Gramm was a very headstrong chairman who had used his power to have his wife appointed to chair the CFTC.

Gramm's support was later critical in the passage of the Commodity Futures Modernization Act of 2000, which kept derivatives transactions, including those involving credit default swaps, free of government regulation. Ironically, Gramm took a job as Vice Chairman for one of the world's largest banks, UBS, after he left the Senate.

In its 2008 coverage of the financial crisis, The Washington Post named Gramm one of seven "Key Players in the Battle over Regulating Derivatives," for having "pushed through several major bills to deregulate the banking and investment industries, including the 1999 Gramm-Leach-Bliley Act that brought down the walls separating the commercial banking and investment banking.

The act is most widely known for repealing portions of the Glass-Steagall Act, also known as the Banking Act of 1933 (48 Stat. 162). The act prohibited commercial banks from engaging in the investment business. It was enacted as an emergency response to the failure of nearly five thousand banks during the Great Depression.

A recent book by Michael Lewis, The Big Short, and the movie based on it, describe how bad the global financial crash was. The book should be required reading for congressmen and federal regulators. Although I lived through this, and witnessed how this travesty violated all principles of open and transparent trading, I had forgotten how bad it was.

The book points out the trillion dollar costs of bailing out our banks, the millions of jobs lost, and the number of people who lost their homes. It left our country more divided because the average working men and women could not understand why the big banks were bailed out and they were not.

I did have the satisfaction of advising my good friend Collin Peterson, then chairman of the House Agriculture Committee, on ways to bring derivatives back under proper regulations.

Peterson had his reform package approved by the House Agriculture Committee well over a year before it was enacted into the law known as the Dodd-Frank Act. We have joked that it should have called the Dodd-Peterson Act. He has noted that the voters in his district have no idea of his role in this landmark legislation.

Since my old client the Chicago Board of Trade had been recently acquired by the CME, I had no conflict of interest. Although I was not in a position to financially benefit from it, I am gratified that two giant futures and derivatives exchanges, the CME headquartered in Chicago and the ICE headquartered in Atlanta, have surpassed all of the world's derivatives and stock exchanges.

They were able to do so because they were the first to adopt computerized trading and phase out the open outcry trading in the futures markets and the specialist system on the stock markets. This was the case because of the strong leadership of two visionary leaders. The first was Leo Melamed at the Chicago Mercantile Exchange. Everyone in the industry refers to him simply as "Leo." He led the little "butter and egg exchange" to become the great CME that eventually overtook and subsumed the larger Chicago Board of Trade that I represented.

Leo's 1996 book, Escape to the Futures, is an inspiring story of his family's escape from the Nazis when he was a 7 year old boy. They had to travel by train from Poland through Siberia to Japan. They were fortunate to leave Japan only a few months before the Japanese bombing of Pearl Harbor. They landed on the West Coast and traveled from there to Chicago. From that point, Leo's remarkable career began. He went to night law school and took a job as a runner on the Chicago Mercantile Exchange (CME), and that was how he was introduced to futures trading

Leo was able to lead the CME to computerization because he was a trading member of the CME as well as its chairman. He never gave up active trading in all of the time he was leading the CME. Tom Donavan was the top-paid executive of the CBOT, but was never a trader or chairman. Therefore, Leo went down in history as perhaps the greatest financial innovator of the twentieth century

Much later, Jeffrey Sprecher, a former energy trader, established the Intercontinental Exchange (ICE). It acquired the New York Stock Exchange.

The Chicago Board of Trade was unable to adapt fast enough because neither Tom Donovan nor anyone else could overcome the opposition of the floor traders on the Chicago Board of Trade. They believed that computerized trading would wipe out their livelihoods. Instead, their failure to adopt computerized trading would wipe out the 159-

year-old Chicago Board of Trade as well as their livelihoods.

In 2015 for the first time there were more derivatives traded in Asia than in the US. This was done because of leadership from Chicago. Both Richard Sandor and Leo spent a lot of time in China, teaching their people about derivatives trading. In fact, my old friend Sandor had his book Good Derivatives translated into Chinese. Since it is the first time I have ever had my name written in Chinese, I keep it on the coffee table in my office.

This American leadership of financial derivatives and stock trading would not have happened had we not created the little agency called the Commodity Futures Trading Commission in 1974.

Unfortunately, Senate Banking Committee Chairman Phil Gramm pushed through Gramm-Leach-Bliley Act, known as the Financial Services Act of 1999. These changes in law were responsible for the Great Recession of 2008, the worst financial crisis since the Great Depression. Gramm was a very headstrong Chairman who had used his power to have his wife appointed to chair the CFTC.

Gramm's support was later critical in the passage of the Commodity Futures Modernization Act of 2000, which kept derivatives transactions, including those involving credit default swaps, free of government regulation.

In its 2008 coverage of the financial crisis, The Washington Post named Gramm one of seven "Key Players In the Battle Over Regulating Derivatives", for having "pushed through several major bills to deregulate the banking and investment industries, including the 1999 Gramm-Leach-Bliley act that brought down the walls separating the commercial banking and investment banking. The Act is most widely known for repealing portions of the Glass-Steagall Act, also known as the Banking Act of 1933 (48 Stat. 162). It was passed by Congress in 1933 and prohibits commercial banks from engaging in the investment business. It was enacted as an emergency response to the failure of nearly 5,000 banks during the Great Depression.

A recent book by Michael Lewis, "The Big Short", and the movie based on it, describes how bad the global financial crash was. The book should be required reading by congressmen and federal regulators. Although I lived through this, and witnessed how this travesty had violated all principles of open and transparent trading, I had forgotten how bad it was.,

The book points out the trillion dollar costs of bailing out our banks, the millions of jobs lost, and the number of people who lost their homes.

I did have the satisfaction of advising my good friend Collin Peterson, then Chairman of the House Agriculture Committee, on ways to bring derivatives back under proper regulations.

Peterson had his reform package approved by the House Agriculture Committee well over a year before it was enacted into the law known as the Dodd-Frank Act. We have joked that it should have called the Dodd-Peterson Act. He has noted that the voters in his district have no idea of his role in this landmark legislation.

Since my old client the Chicago Board of Trade had been acquired by the CME, I had no conflict of interest. Although I was not in a position to financially benefit from it, I have derived great satisfaction from the fact that two giant futures and derivatives exchanges, the CME headquartered in Chicago and the ICE headquartered in Atlanta have surpassed all of the world's derivatives and stock exchanges.

.

They were able to do so because they were the first to adopt computerized trading and phase out the open outcry trading in the futures markets and the specialist system on the stock markets. This was the case because of the strong leadership of two visionary leaders. The first was Leo Melamed at the Chicago Mercantile Exchange. He is only person I know of who everyone in an industry referred to simply by his first name, "Leo". He led the little "butter and egg exchange" to become the great CME that eventually overtook and subsumed the larger Chicago Board of Trade that I represented.

Later, Jeffrey Sprecher, a former energy trader, established the Intercontinental Exchange (ICE). It acquired the New York Stock Exchange. Both Leo and Sprecher were able to do all of this because they were the first to adopt computerized trading. The Chicago Board of Trade was unable to adapt fast enough because neither Tom Donovan nor anyone else could overcome the opposition of the floor traders on the Chicago Board of Trade. They believed that computerized trading would wipe out their livelihoods. Instead their failure to adopt computerized trading would wipe out the 159 year old Chicago Board of Trade as well as their jobs.

None of this would have been possible had we not created the obscure little agency called the Commodity Futures Trading Commission in 1974.

Reagan and Morning in America

On all issues, it didn't take Reagan very long to change my mind about him. He had a great ability to work with a Congress controlled by the opposition party. He and House Speaker Tip O'Neal got along well. Reagan would say, "We are all friends after five o'clock in Washington". He got along better with many Democrats than did Jimmy Carter.

However, I still considered myself a Democrat when Reagan ran for reelection, and I found it impossible to resist the chance to work for the election of Senator John Glenn of Ohio in the Democratic primary in 1984. I led his agriculture issues team and actually had the chance to personally brief him in his Senate office about these issues. My old friend Don Tyson contributed to his campaign and had his son John come up to Washington for a large fundraiser we had for Glenn in the old National Guard Memorial Building.

In addition to being a national hero as the first American astronaut to orbit the earth, Glenn was a superb gentleman. This was demonstrated when he and his wife invited all of the little issue groups who had worked for him out to intimate little dinners in their home in Potomac, Maryland. My little group was the agricultural policy group. My wife and I attended. Most politicians forget to say "thank you" after a losing campaign. The fact that he did not forget says a lot about his character.

After it became apparent that Mondale would be the Democratic nominee, and Glenn dropped out, I was invited to help out in his campaign. Mondale had been the junior senator from Minnesota, serving with Senator Humphrey until he served as Vice President under President Carter.

However, I never warmed up to him as I had to Senator Humphrey. While they were both liberals from Minnesota, Humphrey could give a passionate speech on the Senate floor and not be offensive. He was the only Senator that could arouse the tourists in the gallery to stand up and cheer when he spoke. The Capitol Police would have to tell them to be seated. When Mondale gave a speech, he could be strident, and none of the tourists cheered.

Besides, I had warmed to President Reagan. I had been disenchanted with some of the right wingers who were political appointees in the first Reagan term. They seemed to be opposed to some of the most important programs of the Department of Agriculture, those enacted by Democrats. Among those were the Rural Development Program, which was a proud legislative achievement of both Senator Talmadge and Senator Humphrey.

Also, they seemed intent on undermining the new federal-private sector crop insurance program, whose trade association was and remains a principal client of mine. It is also the program that nations all over the world are copying. Assistant Secretary Frank Naylor, who felt his oats because he was a protégé of Bob Dole, was the worst. When I would meet with him, he would say that all the major members of my trade association were crooks.

This forced me to go to Dick Lyng, the Deputy Secretary of Agriculture, who had been the State Director of Agriculture in California under Governor Reagan. He was a personal friend of Reagan, and led his farm campaign when Reagan ran for President in 1980. Fortunately, Mr. Lyng proved to be a very reasonable and capable man.

Most important, Lyng had the ear of President. I am not sure the crop insurance program would have even survived without him. Lyng was elderly, and he retired after serving in the first term of the Reagan presidency. He agreed to serve as outside member of the board of directors of my client the American Association of Crop Insurers.

While he was only the Deputy Secretary, he had helped get the farm commodity checkoff programs going. This is happened after we helped get the legislation authorizing the National Dairy Board enacted. When it was enacted, the General Counsel of USDA wanted to prohibit the use of outside counsel. Deputy Secretary Lyng was quick to make a decision. He said the government lawyers were too busy with other duties to be able to be able to handle the huge amount of contract work for a board as big as the Dairy Board. That established the precedent for all other checkoff boards to hire outside counsel if they wished.

When Reagan's first term Secretary of Agriculture, John Block, had to resign because he was so far in debt (a situation all too common to farmers), Reagan made a personal appeal to Lyng, as well as to his wife Bethyl, to return as his Secretary of Agriculture in the Reagan second term. He could not resist the personal appeal of his President, and he was appointed Secretary of Agriculture. He served out the remainder of Reagan's second term, and then returned to California. He put his house in McLean, Virginia on the market. Characteristically, he gave the listing to a neighborhood friend who had lost his job. When it didn't sell, he and Bethyl turned to my realtor wife, Sandy, to successfully sell it. We remained close personal friends until his death.

All in all, Lyng was the best Secretary of Agriculture I ever knew or even knew of. When I came to see him at USDA he did not need a lot of staff. He only had one young man present to take notes. When you asked him for something, he would either say yes or no. If he said no, he would explain his reasoning so well that you did not feel bad.

Lyng demonstrated to me one of Reagan's best qualities--he was a generalist who left the details to someone he trusted. In the case of Agriculture, it was his fellow Californian, Dick Lyng. In the case of James Baker, Reagan picked for his Chief of Staff one of his former opponents in the Republican Party. Baker had been the top strategist in trying to secure the Republican nomination for his fellow Texan, George H. W. Bush.

Lyng had the advantage of having served as Assistant Secretary of Agriculture in the Nixon

Administration. He was upset when he was not asked to return for Nixon's second term. He promptly took the job of President of the American Meat Institute, where he served until he was selected as Deputy Secretary by President Reagan.

Lyng's moderation was never more evident than in the case of David Stockman, the Director of the Office of Management and Budget in the Reagan Administration (OMB). Stockman was so extremely conservative that eventually he was fired by Reagan Chief of Staff James Baker after Baker had warned him.

Stockman then wrote a tell-all book. He was a foe of all farm programs. The book characterized Mr. Lyng as the "caretaker of the Welfare State". I bought his book and offered a copy to Lyng. He said "I will not be a part of that SOB selling one more book". However he did agree to borrow the book from me. A few days later, I received the book back in the mail.

After he was fired from the Reagan Administration, Stockman was prosecuted by the SEC for defrauding investors with an investment firm he founded. The suit was later settled for undisclosed terms.

One of Lyng's protégés and his god-daughter was his Assistant Deputy Secretary Anne Venneman. Under my great friend Secretary Madigan, she was appointed Deputy Secretary. She would later become the nation's first woman Secretary of Agriculture in the administration of George W. Bush.

President Reagan was very good at working with Democrats in Congress. As a freshman congressman from rural Texas, Charlie Stenholm was very proud to talk to the President. I remember being in his office when he received a call from President Reagan. Freshman Republicans were not getting those personal calls from Reagan.

Stenholm served for many years with distinction on the House Agriculture Committee. His fondest ambition was to be Chairman of the House Agriculture Committee. Unfortunately, Stenholm's district was eventually dismembered and divided among four adjoining districts. He was a major target of the Tom DeLay-engineered redrawing of Texas congressional districts in 2003. Most of his former territory, including his home in Abilene, was thrown into the heavily Republican Lubbock-based 19th District, represented by Congressman Randy Neugebauer.

His friends were quite concerned, and I traveled to West Texas for an event that I organized for him that was attended by many of my clients. However, there was nothing we could do. He was badly defeated in his race for reelection. We lost a good congressman noted for working across the aisle in a bipartisan manner.

As for the record of President Reagan, he had many victories as well as a few rough patches. His popularity waned a bit before he was shot outside of the Hilton Hotel by the attempted assassin, John Hinckley, Jr. Reagan's press secretary, James Brady, took a bullet in the head that was meant for Reagan. He was partially paralyzed and eventually died from his injuries. As Reagan prayed to God for his own recovery he also prayed for the mixed up young man who had just shot him. There is no better illustration of Reagan's humanity than this.

Reagan staged a heroic recovery after this near death experience. His popularity levels soared after that. Most people would agree that Reagan was a great healer rather than a divider. He had many achievements, such as bringing down the Berlin Wall and the reunification of Germany. When he made his historic speech, "Mr. Gorbachev, tear down your wall", it was characterized as the worst presidential speech in history by one elite historian who people have now forgotten. However, it was lauded by most as one of the best speeches of all time.

Reagan's most enduring legacy is that he did a great job of inspiring our nation and bringing it together. He made us think of our nation as "the shining city on the hill". With him as President, it was possible to forget that Watergate ever happened. I am glad to see his statute greet me every week as I go through Ronald Reagan National Airport.

I am a fan of his speech writer Peggy Noonan, who was responsible for so many of the memorable lines delivered by Reagan. They were his thoughts, but she was responsible for crafting them so well.

Noonan also served as a speechwriter for President George H. W. Bush, who was not as articulate as Reagan. She coined the phrases "a kinder, gentler nation," "a thousand points of light" and "read my lips: no new taxes." She has written books about both Reagan and Bush. I look forward to her weekly columns in the Wall Street Journal.

George H.W. Bush: Defeated by a Loony Third Party Candidate

The first President Bush ran for the job of being President and won primarily on the strength of having served for eight years as the Vice-President for President Reagan. He was not the most eloquent speaker or the most brilliant political strategist. Some in the liberal elite media knocked him as not being intellectual enough for the job. However, he was very honorable, and that goodness came through when you met him and he looked you in the eye. He sought a "kinder gentler nation". It is unquestionable that he tried to unite the county rather than divide it.

It is ironic that Bush was a moderate Republican who probably could not even be elected to state wide office in Texas today. Senator Ted Cruz, who is running for President today, is on another planet from that of George H W Bush or even his son George W. Bush.

Bush was extremely popular after his Desert Storm war to drive Saddam Hussein out of Kuwait. He was wise enough to stop there and not invade Iraq. Unfortunately, the economy took a downturn, and budget deficits soared. Bush had made the famous pledge in his first presidential campaign, "Read my lips. No new

taxes". The fact that he had to violate that
pledge in order to be responsible is widely cited
as the reason he lost his campaign for
reelection.

However, there were two factors that
contributed to Bush's defeat in his bid for
reelection. While Bush was a principled man
who always tried to do the right thing, he was
not very skillful as a politician. He did have a
very skillful young campaign manager who
thrived in the rough and tumble of high stakes
political campaigns. He was Lee Atwater of
South Carolina. Atwater was masterful in
Bush's winning campaign for President. While
Bush was above the fray, Atwater relished
political combat. His strategy was very
successful as they rolled over Governor
Dukakis of Massachusetts in the 1988
presidential race.

Unfortunately, young Atwater developed a brain
tumor and died at the age of 40. As a result, the
Bush forces ran an ineffectual campaign that
failed to utilize the power of the incumbency.
My good friend, former Congressman Ed
Madigan was Bush's Secretary of Agriculture
and like a brother to me. He joined my law firm,
McLeod, Watkinson & Miller, after Bush was
defeated. He lamented to me how poorly the
cabinet members were being utilized in the

campaign. He spoke of being scheduled to make an appearance at a high school along with Lamar Alexander, the Secretary of Education. He said, "Lamar and I talked, and neither one of us knew what we were doing there".

I remember attending the National Republican Convention in Houston in 1992. As a lobbyist for the Chicago Board of Trade I attended both conventions. It was the most dispirited national political convention I ever attended. Pat Buchanan was the first adviser hired by Richard Nixon for his presidential campaign. He worked primarily as an opposition researcher. Buchanan traveled with Richard Nixon throughout the campaigns of 1966 and 1968 as a far right political operative. Fortunately for him, he was not high enough in the Nixon hierarchy to be involved in Watergate.

After Nixon's fall, Buchanan had high visibility as a right-wing television commentator and author of some books. On the 25th anniversary of the Watergate, he wrote "Watergate was indeed a coup. It was the overthrow of an elected president by a media and political elite he had routed in a 49-state landslide the like of which America had never seen".

In 1992, Buchanan ran for the nation's highest office in his own right. He challenged Bush from the right wing prior to the convention. Because he had some following in the Republican Party, it was considered important to pacify him. In an effort to avoid a split in the Republican Party, the Bush forces brokered a deal where Buchanan would endorse Bush in exchange for the opportunity to make a keynote speech to the convention.

It did not work. The mood was downbeat, and women delegates were dispirited. This was a beginning of the culture wars, and feminists were insulted by the comments of Buchanan. Even my wife, who is not a strong feminist, was very negative about the entire convention. My client Tom Donovan, President of the Chicago Board of Trade, said we were wasting our time and money being there. It was the most dispiriting National Convention since the Democratic Convention attended in Atlanta in 1988 when Dukakis was nominated.

Even then, Bush would have won had it not been for a scrawny little rich guy from Texas. Ross Perot mounted a third party campaign. He sounded like a wacko to many people, but tapped into the votes of the disenchanted part of the electorate, much like tea party candidates do today.

Perot tried to appear non-partisan by hiring Hamilton Jordan, Jimmy Carter's former chief of staff, and Wayne Rollins, a political operative for Ronald Reagan, to manage his campaign. He made it clear that he would spend enough of his own money to get elected. In fact, he spent $67 million, which would be $107 million in today's dollars, which is more than the $100 million that Donald Trump has promised to spend on his own election for the Presidency in 2016.

In the end, all that Perot did was ensure the election of Bill Clinton. Because Perot got 19 per cent of the vote, most of it from Republican voters who were fiscal conservatives, Clinton was able to win the election with only 43 per cent of the popular vote. Bush, the quintessential nice guy, lost.

The Horrors of War

President Bush 41 had been a bomber pilot in World War II. He had joined the Navy at age eighteen and his airplane was shot down in the ocean when he was twenty. Both he and George McGovern were members of what Tom Brokaw called "The Greatest Generation" in his best-selling book. I bought a copy of this book for one of my uncles who participated in the Normandy invasion.

George McGovern experienced war as a bomber pilot under fire over Nazi-occupied Europe in World War II. He earned a Distinguished Flying Cross for crash-landing his damaged Liberator, the Dakota Queen II, on an island in the Adriatic Sea.

It is interesting that both George H. W. Bush and George McGovern experienced the horrors of war firsthand but took away different lessons from it. Bush had an aversion to war but believed that it was sometimes necessary to go to war to protect our vital national interests. McGovern became a peace activist and ultimately was a Democratic candidate for president against Richard Nixon in 1972. I got to know him personally because he was a Democratic member of the Senate Agriculture

Committee both before and after he ran for president.

Regardless of this, McGovern was a great human being who never took himself too seriously. He dealt courageously with his share of personal tragedies. He reached out to me when he saw I was personally devastated by the Senate Ethics Committee hearings about Talmadge. It is no wonder that I tried to help him get reelected to the Senate in South Dakota.

I remember traveling to Chicago with McGovern to visit the Chicago Board of Trade. He said that he always liked Chicago because it was, in the words of poet Carl Sandberg, "the city with big shoulders."

McGovern suffered his greatest personal defeat when his daughter Terry died in the snows of Madison, Wisconsin, in 1995. Characteristically, he wrote a book about her and created a charity in her name. It is no wonder that I worked hard for his campaign when he ran for reelection to the Senate. Unfortunately, he was defeated. He then opened a bed and breakfast in Connecticut. After that, he wrote an op-ed piece for The Wall Street Journal saying he had been wrong to want to put too many regulations on small businesses.

I have noticed that my two uncles, who fought in the Normandy invasion, never talked about what they did in World War II. Later, our best friends in the Washington area would become the Hirsch family. The patriarch was Brigadier General Hirsch, who had served in three wars—World War II, the war in Korea, and the war in Vietnam. When we would have our annual Thanksgiving dinner, I would propose a toast to him as my hero. He would demur and say he only did what anybody else would have done.

I later got to know Max Cleland, who became a triple amputee in the war in Vietnam. He was a young lieutenant who was one year younger than me. He was named administrator of the Veterans Administration by President Carter. He later went back to Georgia and was elected secretary of state, which is only a ministerial job.

When Cleland ran for the US Senate, he had his first Washington fundraiser in my office. I will never forget that McGovern came to it and wrote a personal check out of his own account.

When he was sworn into the Senate, there was a large celebration for him that was attended by Hollywood celebrities such as Carroll O'Connor.

When he began his service in the Senate, I attended a reception for him in the Georgetown home of Democratic elders Averell and Pamela Harriman. Harriman's service went back to Franklin D. Roosevelt and Harry Truman.

Cleland remained a friend while he was in the Senate. I remember running into him once at the airport, and my young son asked, "Where are your legs?" I even tried to play matchmaker for this single senator. My wife and I had him to dinner at our home, and we introduced him to my wife's best friend, who was single. She had read his inspiring book "Strong at the Broken Places".

Unfortunately, Cleland never got the hang of being a senator and was defeated in his race for reelection. He then became a peace activist who demonstrated outside the Texas ranch of President George W. Bush.

Bill Clinton-- Brilliant Politician Tarnished by Grave Ethical Flaws

The first time I ever met Clinton was when he was a young governor from Arkansas at a meeting on world trade in Chicago, he obviously had star quality. The press cameras focused on him.

William Jefferson Clinton is one of the most gifted politicians who was ever elected President. He had very good instincts for public service, but his personal morals were deplorable. From my perch as an agricultural lawyer and lobbyist, I had a chance to observe this first hand. I knew that Clinton had too many responsibilities to devote much time to farm policy, although he came from Arkansas, a poor rural state that depended on federal farm programs.

I was able to develop a close personal friendship with a rice farmer from Arkansas who had been named Clinton's agricultural adviser in the White House. With him there, farm programs got a lot of attention. He is Marion Berry, and both his personal morals and his public service character were impeccable. Marion explained to me Clinton's insatiable need to have people like him. When Governor Clinton would come to visit Marion, his young son would be jealous. Clinton would go out of his way to win the kid over.

Like any other President, Clinton made a lot of appointments that supported his agenda or had their own personal agendas that were consistent with his. Fortunately, his first appointment for the Secretary of Agriculture was Mike Espy, a black congressman from Mississippi. Espy is the first and only black Secretary of Agriculture we have ever had. He was dedicated to improving the lot of the poor farmers of all colors from his state.

Under Espy's leadership, the Clinton Administration was able to come up with another billion dollars a year in the budget baseline to improve the crop insurance program and make it viable. The Federal Crop Insurance Reform Act of 1994 made it possible to insure the basic commodities at a level that would make it possible to phase out the huge off-the-budget expense of ad-hoc disaster payments.

With the support of that admirable public servant, OMB Director Leon Panetta, the $1 billion was made available in the budget baseline on the recognition that this much or more has been saved by eliminating ad-hoc disaster payments. This calculation was ultimately vindicated as the crop insurance program eventually made annual off-budget emergency bailouts unnecessary. As proof of the validity of crop insurance concept, India and other countries all over the world have attempted to emulate our American crop insurance program.

Unfortunately, Espy was forced to resign because of an ethics violation resulted in a relentless investigation by an Independent Counsel, Donald Smalz. Since Espy was so visible in creating the first successful national crop insurance program, Smalz looked hard at our industry. As the representative of the crop insurance industry, I had to visit the independent Counsel's office more than once and turn over all of my records.

Fortunately, the only crop insurance company implicated in any wrongdoing was a rogue insurance company that was not a member of my trade association, the American Association of Crop Insurers. The chief executive of this company, John Hemingson, had former Congressman Tony Coelho represent him rather than my trade association. Hemingson was convicted and sent to jail. Ultimately, he was pardoned by President Clinton.

Another casualty of the Smalz prosecution was prominent Agriculture lobbyist and former

Reagan campaign aide Jim Lake. He was forced to plead guilty for making an illegal campaign contribution to Espy's brother, a local Mississippi politician.

As for Espy, he was ultimately acquitted at trial. I have thought more than once about the irony of Espy being forced out of office by some minor slip-ups in violating the gift regulations (he let my old friend Don Tyson buy him some tickets to a football game), while President Clinton was able to avoid the same fate although he was guilty of much greater transgressions.

After Espy was forced out, I had grave concerns about whether the next appointee would be as good. Indeed, by the time the landmark crop insurance legislation was passed, Secretary Glickman was in place. A large bill-signing ceremony was held in the White House Rose Garden. Glickman gave a mundane speech that is standard at these events.

Then William Jefferson Clinton got up and gave one of the best farm speeches that I have ever heard. He invoked the name of his political namesake, Thomas Jefferson, who he reminded us, was a farmer. He said, "The only problem with Jefferson was that he thought that everybody ought to be farmers". Afterwards, he stood there shaking the hands of everyone who went through the receiving line. I even went back through a second time to get a personally autographed photo for my young son. Consistent with his political operation, I received the photo in the mail a few days later.

It was very unfortunate that Clinton's personal ethical failings prevented him from going down as one of our greatest presidents. It was quite ironic that he was ultimately impeached by the House of Representatives after being investigated by the Independent Counsel's office, the same office that brought down Secretary Espy. Espy was only guilty of petty indiscretions compared to those of Clinton.

Clinton possessed incredible political skills, and his two terms as President were good for the nation in many respects. The economy was good, and he produced two balanced budgets, the last time this has been done. He did so by his strategy of triangulation –balancing the interests of his own party with the interests of Republicans. He had the latitude to do this before he was impeached. After that he had to hew to the partisan line of Senate Democrats who votes he had needed in order not be convicted in the Senate.

Clinton's various scandals and affairs were extremely polarizing. A good book by Gail Sheehy, "Hillary's Choice" does a good job of chronicling the many scandals that dogged the Clinton Presidency. Sheehy, a writer for Vanity Fair, had become a good friend and confidante of Hillary Clinton. Hillary's relationship with Bill reached a low point during the Monica Lewinsky scandal when Clinton said on national television, "I did not have sex with that woman".

Of course Clinton became a target of Special Prosecutor Kenneth Starr only because he was investigating the Whitewater scandal in Arkansas. This is a case of a fraudulent land deal in which the Madison Savings and Loan went bankrupt. The Clintons were partners and investors in the land deal, and Hillary was the attorney of James B. McDougal and the Madison Guaranty Savings & Loan. Contrary to popular belief, the Special Prosecutor's probe was not prompted by the many allegations of sexual harassment made by Arkansas women such as Paula Hawkins and Gennifer Flowers.

The Independent Counsel's Office was created by a Democratic Congress bent on curbing the abuses of executive power by Richard Nixon in the Watergate scandal. The prosecutor, who was appointed by a special panel of the United States Court of Appeals for the District of

Columbia Circuit, could investigate allegations of any misconduct, with an unlimited budget and no deadline, and could be dismissed only by the Attorney General for "good cause" or by the special panel of the court when the independent counsel's task was completed. As the president could not dismiss those investigating the executive branch it was felt that the independence of the office would ensure impartiality of any reports presented to Congress.

There have been many critics of this law, including conservative Supreme Court Justice Antonin Scalia. Many argued the new Independent Counsel's office was a sort of "fourth branch" of government that had virtually unlimited powers and was answerable to no one. However, the constitutionality of the new office was ultimately upheld in the 1988 Supreme Court case Morrison v. Olson.

Finally the Congress had enough of this office, with an unlimited budget and no timeline. The law was not extended in 1999, and it was replaced by the U.S. Department of Justice Special Counsel.

However, this did not come soon enough to save Clinton. He became the only President since Andrew Johnson to be impeached by the

House of Representatives. Richard Nixon resigned before the House of Representatives could impeach him when informed by the Senate Republican Leader, Hugh Scott, that the Senate would convict him. When Scott retired from the Senate, he would become my law partner in the firm of Scott, Harrison & McLeod.

Ironically, the actions that brought about Clinton's impeachment were not the sexual trysts with his employees. He was impeached for one count of perjury and one count of obstruction of justice. If one looks at the history of Lyndon Johnson's years in Congress and the White House, it would seem that Clinton was not as bad as Johnson as far as having several affairs with women he employed. Nor had he used his public office to build up the tremendous wealth that Johnson had.

Even after the impeachment, Clinton left office after 8 years with the highest end-of-office approval rating of any Democratic U.S. president since World War II. This is amazing, but it is a tribute to Clinton's enormous political skills. One wonders what a great political legacy he could have left if he had not had such huge moral failings. Unfortunately, his tenure served to divide the nation rather than bring us together.

George W. Bush: Republican Moderate who was forced to be a Wartime President.

George W. Bush got into politics because he was the scion of a famous family. His grandfather, Prescott Bush, had been a Senator from Connecticut. His father had President for one term. Like his father, he tried his hand as an oil wildcatter. When that played out, he had the opportunity to be the President of the Texas Rangers. In a few years, his backers were able to sell the franchise for enough money to set him up for life. He then was elected Governor of Texas.

 We will never know how Bush would have done in normal times. We do know he ran as a "compassionate conservative".

These were not normal times. On September 11, 2001 our homeland was attacked for the first time in history. First, the twin towers in New York were attacked by airplanes that were hijacked by Muslim terrorists. This would change our country and the world forever.

I was sitting calmly in my office that overlooks the Capitol buildings. Someone rushed in and said I should turn on my television. I did, and the commentator said it appeared that one of the towers in New York had been hit by an airplane. The initial reports indicated that it was a small airplane that had gotten off course. Then another airplane struck the second tower, and all hell broke loose.

We knew we were in big trouble. However, I told everyone in my office that we should stay calm. Shortly thereafter, there was another airplane that ran into the fortress-like Pentagon, which lies below the home I lived in on Arlington Ridge Road.

We were still trying to remain calm. Little did we know that the terrorists had high jacked a third airplane that was headed straight for the U.S. Capitol, only a long block away from my office. I urged everyone to sit tight and not panic. Had I known that there was another high jacked airplane headed straight for the Capitol, .I would have urged everyone to run as far as possible. Fortunately, some patriots stormed the cockpit and the armed hijackers. Instead of the Capitol, the airplane went down in Shanksville, Pennsylvania.

President Bush responded decisively to this, the first ever attack against the American Homeland. We promptly went to war in Iraq and Afghanistan and began hunting down Osama Ben Laden and his band of terrorists. Unfortunately, this defined Bush's presidency, and Ben Laden was not killed until his successor, President Obama, was campaigning for his reelection to a second term.

Vice President Joe Biden coined the campaign slogan, "Osama Ben Laden is dead and General Motors is alive". So much of life and politics is pure luck. Bush had forcefully put in motion the means of killing Osama Be Laden, but his successor, Obama, got the credit for it.

Unlike his father, George W. Bush listened to faulty advice from some of his advisers and invaded Iraq. History has shown that the impact of this was to destabilize the Middle East and pave the way for Muslim extremists. It made him an unpopular President by the time he left office.

The book "Destiny and Power: The American Odyssey of George Herbert Walker Bush" by Jon Meacham is based on the personal diaries of George and Barbara Bush. In this book Bush reveals that his son George W. Bush was misled by the advice of Vice President Dick Cheney and Secretary of Defense Donald Rumsfeld. One does not need to read the book to remember that Rumsfeld predicted that our troops would be welcomed as conquering heroes by the citizens of Iraq.

This unsuccessful attempt to transplant American democracy to the Middle East has resulted in over 6,000 American deaths in Iraq and Afghanistan. The number of wounded warriors is far greater than that. The following is reported by the Wounded Warrior Project that continually advertises for private donations:

"With advancements in battlefield medicine and body armor, an unprecedented percentage of service members are surviving severe wounds or injuries. For every US soldier killed in World Wars I and II, there were 1.7 soldiers wounded. In Operation Iraqi Freedom and Operation Enduring Freedom, for every US soldier killed, seven are wounded. Combined, over 48,000 servicemen and women have been physically injured in the recent military conflicts."

"In addition to the physical wounds, it is estimated as many as 400,000 service members live with the invisible wounds of war including combat-related stress, major depression, and post-traumatic stress disorder. Another 320,000 are believed to have experienced a traumatic brain injury while on deployment."

Unfortunately, the Middle East is more unstable and dangerous than any time in history. The terrorist organization ISIS has mounted terrorist attacks all over the world and has successfully recruited young men and women from within our own country.

Barack Obama--Opportunity for a Post Racial Society Wasted

Barack Obama was elected President as an unknown quantity. In Illinois he had only been an obscure state senator who avoided taking difficult votes. In the U.S. Senate, he was a first term Senator who again tried hard to make friends and avoid making enemies. He even became a good personal friend of perhaps the most conservative Republican member of the Senate, Tom Coburn of Oklahoma. As someone who had represented the Chicago Board of Trade for three decades, I knew Chicago Senators and Congressman. I found no one who both knew him and supported him.

The thing that Obama did well was talk. Boy, could he make a speech!

At the suggestion of a journalist friend, I bought the first edition of his autobiography, "Dreams from My Father". This was the first edition, before he was famous and was running for President.

What I read really scared me! The father he was referring to was a Kenyan socialist and ant-colonialist. The father had come to Hawaii on a scholarship as a grad student in college and married a young woman who promptly got pregnant. That union produced a son they named Barak Obama. The father soon moved on to another young woman after he got a chance for a scholarship at the much more prestigious Harvard. He eventually moved back to Kenya and got into Kenyan politics.

Obama's father was a dedicated socialist and ant-colonialist. However, he soon became frustrated and isolated because the father of modern Kenya, Jomo Kenyatta, soon ditched his socialism and anti-colonialism. He found that it didn't work. Thus, the elder Obama could not get a job. Instead he became a drunk and died an early death in an auto accident.

When I read this, I was alarmed. I was afraid that if we elected a President he who would try to carry out the dreams of his deceased socialist and anti-colonialist father it would be wrong for our nation.

Thus, I was moved to get more heavily involved in a Presidential campaign than I had been since those of Jimmy Carter. I had always admired John McCain as a war hero and patriot. I became a early supporter, and donated several thousand dollars of my personal money, even in the Republican Primary, when most pundits gave him no chance.

I stuck with McCain even when his lack of understanding of the economy during the Great Recession doomed his chances. My efforts to help him were also impaired when he went out of his way to insult my clients, the farmers and ranchers of the nation. He had always been opposed to farm programs. Of course, his selection a ditzy young woman named Sarah Palin as his vice presidential running mate helped seal his fate. In an interview with Katie Couric, she could not even say what newspapers she read.

Senator McCain knew nothing about agriculture and only knew he was against all farm programs. Even worse, he admitted he didn't understand the economy. In 20080, the year of our worst economic meltdown since the Great Depression, that was deadly. I urgently pressed a friend who was working full time in the McCain campaign to have him make an announcement that he would appoint Mitt Romney as his Secretary of the Treasury and economic czar. Certainly, Romney understood the economy. Unfortunately, my suggestion was never taken.

Given the performance of Obama during two terms, I know I made the right decision to at least try to help McCain. The country is more polarized than at any time during my lifetime. We have always had a right wing and a left wing. Obama has embraced the far left wing. In the process, he created the Tea Party. In our political system, as in Isaac Newton's third law of physics, every action provokes an opposite and equal reaction. An extreme action by the left wing seems to promote an equally extreme reaction by the right wing. An extreme action by the right wing provokes the same kind of reaction from the left wing.

An overriding reason that white voters supported Obama in large enough numbers to get him elected twice was that they wanted to demonstrate that white racism was dead. Unfortunately, race relations have gotten a lot worse during his time in office. Beginning with the Trayvon Martin shooting in Florida his rhetoric has been inflammatory. Since Obama did not have an authentic black experience growing up, he chose as his advisor on race relations Al Sharpton, who has a long history of race baiting (Tawana Brawley and "kill the Jew"). Racial animosity and crime reached a new level this year in cities such as Baltimore and Chicago.

Unfortunately, Obama's extreme positions polarized Congress. In his first term, he had a Democratic majority in both houses. However, in his second term, Republicans have a majority in both houses of Congress. I have met Congresswoman Pelosi several times. She is very pleasant person, and she has worked hard to keep her caucus together. However, President Obama has set the agenda for the Democratic Party. She has felt it is her responsibility, as the House Democratic leader, to rally her members behind the Obama agenda. Moreover, she represents San Francisco, one of the most liberal Congressional districts in the nation. , so she has no problem being reelected. Unfortunately, her following the Obama agenda has made the House a very partisan place.

House Speakers --Jim Wright, Tom Foley, Newt Gingrich, Denny Hastert, Nancy Pelosi, and John Boehner

In the history of the Senate, civil discourse has been a hallmark of the Senate until recent years. My old mentor, Robert C. Byrd of West Virginia, was the keeper of the traditions of the Senate. He was totally non-partisan about it. Republican senators have told me that when they came in as freshman senators, Byrd would sit with them for hours on the Senate floor explaining the rules and the traditions of the Senate.

Unfortunately, the House did not quite have that tradition. When I was a young man, Jim Wright of Texas became Speaker of the House. He brought to the office a hard partisan edge that eventually backfired and brought him down. Wright came out of the tough Texas political school led by his mentor, Lyndon Johnson. Moreover, this was the post-Watergate period when a new standard of ethics applied.

Moreover, he was not as shrewd as his mentor. He was accused of petty financial improprieties in avoiding the House gift limitations. The allegation was that he did that in two ways. First, he hired his wife, Betty, and gave her perks. Second, he had lobbyists with interests before the House make large bulk purchases of his book, "Reflections of a Public Man". A lobbyist friend of mine had his client make a very large purchase of them.

To make matters even worse for him, the press published stories about his main aide, John Mack, who had brutally assaulted a young woman who worked for him 16 years earlier. Wright helped him get paroled after only 27 months in prison and again gave him a job in his office.

After the House Ethics Committee opened an investigation prompted by a petition filed by Congressman Newt Gingrich, Wright resigned from the speakership. This traumatic change in the House Leadership began a new era of partisanship to the House.

As a response to this scandal, House Democrats replaced Wright with Tom Foley of Washington State, one of the finest gentlemen I have ever known. He was always very gentlemanly as well as very learned. As with Wright, his wife Heather worked in his office, but she was a volunteer and was unpaid. She was a dear friend of mine who tried hard to help me save a young woman, wife and mother, in my office who ultimately died of anorexia.

I had gotten to know him well when he was the Chairman of the House Agriculture Committee. He and my close friend, Illinois Republican Congressman Ed Madigan, worked together seamlessly. I happened to be in Madigan's office when he had just lost the race to become the Republican whip to this young upstart, Newt Gingrich, by two votes. Foley called Madigan to express his condolences.

Unfortunately, Foley fell victim to a term limits movement in Washington State. During his time in the House, Foley repeatedly opposed state efforts to impose term limits on Washington State's elected federal officials. He won the support of the state's voters to reject term limits in a 1991 referendum. However, in 1992, a term limit ballot initiative was approved by the state's voters.

Foley brought suit, properly challenging the constitutionality of a state law setting eligibility requirements on federal offices. Foley won his suit, with federal courts declaring that states did not have the authority under the United States Constitution to limit the terms of federal officeholders.

However, in Foley's bid for a 16th term in the House, his Republican opponent, George Nethercutt, used the issue against him, properly citing the caption of the federal case brought by Foley, "Foley against the People of the State of Washington". Nethercutt vowed that if elected, he would not serve more than three terms in the House.

Although friends like me worked hard to raise funds for Foley's reelection, he was defeated for reelection in 1994, the first Speaker since 1862 to be defeated in his race for reelection. President Clinton then appointed him Ambassador to Japan, and I did not see much of him and Heather after that.

After Nethercutt defeated Foley in a close race, he forgot his pledge and served for an undistinguished 5 terms before running unsuccessfully for the Senate against Patty Murray. After that defeat, he became a lobbyist and consultant.

Newt Gingrich

Also in 1994, Newt Gingrich led the Republicans to a 54 seat pickup in the House and became Speaker. In 1995 he became the first Republican Speaker of the House in 50 years. His stormy tenure would sharply accelerate the trend toward harsh partisanship that began years earlier by Jim Wright, and interrupted by the gentlemanly Tom Foley. I remember that some of Gingrich's Democratic colleagues in the Georgia House Delegation were very disturbed by Gingrich openly campaigning against them. This just wasn't done before Gingrich did it.

After the 1994 mid-term elections, Newt Gingrich began his stormy tenure as Speaker of the House. Most of the legislative items in his well-publicized "Contract with America" were passed by the House, and many became law. His term as Speaker was marked by his opposition to many of Clinton's policies, which led to a budget showdown, government shutdowns, and acrimonious impeachment proceedings.

As reported by Howard Kurtz in the Daily Beast, "it was also a period of extreme volatility, serial charges of unethical conduct by Gingrich, and a management style so disorganized and unpredictable that within three years, his own lieutenants tried to depose him in a chaotic coup. By the time he was forced out in 1998, many former members say they were terrified to open up the newspaper in the morning, fearful of what he had said or done that could cause them political heartburn."

His four years in the Speakership created a hyper partisan atmosphere that would cripple the legitimate and traditional functioning of the House for years. When he mounted a bid for the Republican Presidential nomination in 2012, few of his former colleagues in the House would support him.

Despite Gingrich's "management by chaos" he and President Clinton managed some major accomplishments. These included an agreement on welfare reform, a capital gains tax cut, and a budget deal that led to four straight balanced budgets. Most of these accomplishments were before the impeachment of Clinton in the case of his affair with his intern, Monica Lewinsky. Gingrich would have been wise to have adhered to the biblical injunction of Jesus in John 8.5 in delivering the adulterous woman, "Let any who is without sin be the first to cast a stone at her."

Unfortunately for Gingrich, he was brought down by charges of his violation of House Ethics rules and heavy Republican losses in the House. He resigned from Congress in 1999 to be replaced by Congressman Bob Livingston of Louisiana. Livingston's term never actually happened.

Hustler Magazine publisher Larry Flint was offended by the pious treatment of Clinton by Republicans. He offered a reward of one million dollars for each unflattering story about the sexual activity of a Republican congressman. The reward produced evidence of Livingston's illicit affairs with several women. Suddenly, Hustler was setting the political agenda of Congress. Livingston resigned his seat in Congress and became a Washington lobbyist.

It was ironic that all of this took place while the House was preparing to impeach President Clinton. Despite the fact that they did impeach him, Gingrich was gone from the House by the time that happened.

In the 1996 presidential election, Clinton was re-elected, receiving 49.2 percent of the popular vote over Republican Bob Dole (40.7 percent of the popular vote) and Reform candidate Ross Perot (8.4 percent of the popular vote). He became the first Democratic incumbent since Franklin D. Roosevelt to be elected President more than once.

After the 1998 elections, the House voted to impeach Clinton, based on alleged acts of perjury and obstruction of justice related to the Lewinsky scandal. This made Clinton the only the second United States President to be impeached, and only the third for whom the full House had considered such proceedings.

The trial in the United States Senate began right after the seating of the 106th Congress in 1999. The Republicans began with 55 senators. A two-thirds vote, or 67 senators, was required to remove Clinton from office. Fifty senators voted to remove Clinton on the obstruction of justice charge and 45 voted to remove him on the perjury charge. No Democrat voted guilty on either charge. Thus, Clinton survived and served out his second term.

The House Republicans scurried around to find someone to take the job of the Speaker of the House, third in line for the Presidency, which is the most powerful job in the world. Both Tom Delay and Dick Armey were considered too toxic. They finally settled on Denny Hastert, a little known congressman from Illinois. The rationale seemed to be that at least he was a straight guy who had no baggage. Hastert, a former high school teacher and wrestling coach, was assumed to be as straight as they come. There was only some concern about the Majority Whip Tom Delay, known as "the hammer". Some people were concerned that Hastert would merely be a puppet for Delay.

Hastert did serve as a non-controversial and well-liked Speaker for 8 years. He consistently supported the policies of President George W.

Bush. He resigned from the Speakership and from Congress when Republicans lost control of the House in 2006. He became a lobbyist with the Washington law firm Dickstein Shapiro for a few years.

However, in 2015 Hastert was forced to plead guilty to a money laundering charge in because he had paid $1.7 million in blackmail to a former male student of his when he was a high school wrestling coach and teacher before entering politics. He now goes down in history as a convicted criminal. Never in the history of our nation has the office of Speaker of the House gone through such a turbulent period as that 10 year period beginning with Newt Gingrich in 1996 and ending with the resignation of Dennis Hastert in 2006.

As it turned out, Tom Delay would serve as Majority Whip only until he was forced out of the House. He was convicted in 2010 of money laundering and conspiracy charges related to illegal campaign finance activities aimed at helping Republican candidates for Texas state office in the 2002 elections.

However, in 2013, a Texas Court of Appeals panel acquitted DeLay when it overturned his conviction. This decision was affirmed by the Texas Court of Criminal Appeals on October 1,

2014. DeLay had three years from that date, i.e. until October 1, 2017, to file any lawsuits for wrongful action.

Subsequently, Gingrich authored several books (70 and still counting). He has stayed involved in politics, serving as a political commentator for Fox News and a consultant for various conservative think tanks. He established several for profit corporations that provide him and his wife Callista (a former Chief Clerk of the House Agriculture Committee) with good incomes. On May 2011, Gingrich announced he would seek the Republican nomination for president in 2012. He had some early success in the Republican primaries, but quickly faded.

While Gingrich's political career ended badly, he achieved several political accomplishments. He negotiated two balanced budgets with President Clinton, the last time this has been done

Another was a curb on regulatory excess. He pushed through Congress the Congressional Review Act, which enabled Congress to cancel, on an expedited basis, regulations it deemed excessive. He helped my small client, the United Egg Producers, which was headquartered in Atlanta.. The Federal Trade

Commission had greatly expanded its regulatory authority under Carter appointee Mike Pertchuk. Mike was something of a regulatory zealot.

The FTC began an investigation of UEP for violating the anti-trust law, and the little trade association did not have the funds to fight it. It was incredible that this could happen to one of the most competitive industries on the planet. Since they didn't have the budget to fight this, we appealed to our Georgia Congressman, Newt Gingrich. The UEP newsletter immediately reported we had met with Gingrich and he promised to help us. FTC got the message and quickly, dropped the investigation.

There is no doubt that Gingrich is one of the most brilliant political leaders we have ever seen, but he had a very confrontational, divisive, and chaotic style. He will not go down in history as one of our greatest Speakers of the House, only one of the most controversial.

John Boehner

In many respects John Boehner personifies the American dream. He grew up the 2nd of 12 children over a bar in Cincinnati. His father was a bar owner and John started working there at age 8. He then worked at several jobs, including that of janitor. His siblings still have blue collar jobs. When he met the girl who became his wife, Debbie, she convinced him to get a college education. Thus, Boehner became the first member of his family to go to college.

In the presidential election year of 2008, the House and Senate, as well as the Presidency came under Democratic control. Nancy Pelosi of California became the first woman to be named Speaker of the House. She held that position during the first term of President Obama. When Obama was reelected in 2012, she lost that position and became House Democratic Leader while John Boehner became Speaker.

Boehner's rise is a classic Horatio Alger story. When Boehner graduated from college he went to work in a plastics company and eventually became its president. As he got more successful he got involved in politics. He was successful enough to accumulate a modest fortune. This enabled him to serve comfortably in the House without the financial pressures of other young members who were maintaining a home in Washington as well as in their district while raising a young family.

During his freshman year, Boehner was a member of the "Gang of Seven" which was involved in bringing media attention to the House banking scandal and the House post office while working for reform. They engaged in such stunts as walking into the House Chamber with a paper bag covering their heads. Some House members, including Gingrich, were accused of kiting checks. The uncovering of these scandals did bring 70 Democrats down, the most notable of which was Dan Rostenkowski, who had been chairman of the House Ways and Means Committee, the most powerful committee in the House.

Along with some other members, Rostenkowski was accused of heading a conspiracy to launder Post Office money through stamps and postal vouchers. There is some doubt that he even knew what was going on. Powerful members of Congress usually leave these details to trusted staff. After expensive legal proceedings, Rostenkowski pleaded guilty in 1996 to mail fraud and was sentenced to 18 months in prison.

The worst thing that Rostenkowski was guilty of was using House Post Office Funds to pay for Kennedy Rockers that he loved to give to his friends in Illinois. He had been close to Jack

Kennedy and would regularly visit his widow Jaqueline Kennedy, after President Kennedy was assassinated. Of course, I am biased because he was a great friend of my client, the Chicago Board of Trade.

Rostenkowski was pardoned by President Clinton in 1998, and his Chicago friends never deserted him for the rest of his life. It has always been the Chicago way to take care of their own.

In the end, Rostenkowski once lamented to a friend, "I'm going to jail for sending a guy a rocking chair."

In his commentary titled: "The Rules Kept Changing; Dan Rostenkowski Didn't", Pulitzer Prize winning columnist Mike Royko, a frequent Rostenkowski critic, wrote "Nobody should be taking pleasure from Rostenkowski's misfortune. Not unless you have never, ever, broken even a minor law and gotten away with it, fudged a bit on your taxes or violated any of the Ten Commandments.' "Only a few decades ago, none of this would have been happening. That's because the rules changed. Most of the things he was nailed for would have been legal and common or, at worst, nickel-dime offenses when he began his career in Congress." Royko also questioned the motives of federal prosecutors, "Rostenkowski was a big political fish-the kind of trophy that an ambitious federal prosecutor loves to stuff and hang on his wall...That's what did Rostenkowski in – a federal prosecutor's personal ambitions."

In a 1998 interview with John F. Kennedy, Jr. for George Magazine, Rostenkowski estimated the government spent over $20 million on his case. "Not many people in this country can counter resources like that, and I'm not one of them. I couldn't finance the fight any longer".

This was all painfully reminiscent for me of what happened to Talmadge. The Senator lost his Senate seat because of the investigation of him by the Senate Ethics Committee. However he was never charged with a crime or went to jail.

Boehner, along with Newt Gingrich and several other Republican lawmakers, was one of the engineers of the "Contract with America". This helped Republicans win the 1994 congressional elections during which they won the majority in Congress for the first time in four decades.

Serving through the tumultuous years of Gingrich's leadership was valuable to Boehner because it taught him the dangers of charting an extremist course. From 1995 to 1999, Boehner served as House Republican

Conference Chairman, which is the party caucus for Republicans in the House of Representatives. In this post, he was the fourth-ranking House Republican, behind Gingrich, Majority Leader Dick Armey and Majority Whip Tom Delay.

Boehner lost out in the House Republican leadership after a failed coup against Gingrich. He then served as Chairman of the Education and Labor Committee, where he worked successfully with Senator Ted Kennedy for the passage of the No Child Left Behind Act of 2001. This legislation was signed by President George W. Bush. Boehner has said that it was his "proudest achèvement" in two decades of public service. Boehner was friends with Kennedy, also a Roman Catholic, and every year they chaired fundraisers for cash-strapped Catholic schools.

I got to know Boehner because he was a member of the House Agriculture Committee. He was a strong supporter of the "Freedom to Farm Act" which was a creation of my good friend Pat Roberts, Chairman of the House Agriculture Committee at the time. This law moved our farm programs away from government controls and toward the free market.

Boehner was an irreverent young congressman while Ed Madigan was the ranking Republican on the House Agriculture Committee. Madigan had gone on to be Secretary of Agriculture in the Administration of the first President Bush. He joined my law firm McLeod, Watkinson & Miller after George H. W. Bush was defeated. He and I would go by Boehner's office. Boehner would say, "Hello, Ed, I see you are dyeing your hair now".

Unfortunately, Madigan died of cancer in his mid-fifties. He was as nonpartisan in death as well as in life, Illinois. I drove from Chicago with Kika de la Garza, Democratic Chairman of the House Agriculture Committee, to Madigan's home town, Lincoln, Illinois. This town was established by Abraham Lincoln. There was a huge funeral for him in Bloomington, Illinois. Congressman Bob Michel, the House Republican leader, sang the Irish ballad "Danny Boy". Dick Durbin, who is now the second ranking Democrat in the Senate, was crying as he walked out of the church.

Boehner has continued to demonstrate the ability to work with most Republicans and certain Democrats on many key issues. One such person is my good friend Collin Peterson, who was Chairman and is now Ranking Democrat of the House Agriculture Committee.

Sadly, Peterson is one of the few moderate to conservative Democrats left in the House. Boehner has always told me that he and Peterson came into the House at the same time, and that he both liked and respected Peterson. I know that the feeling is mutual.

Boehner is a very practical guy who just wants get the job done. That is a part of being a completely self-made man. Like other self-made men, he knew that you get ahead only by learning from your mistakes and adjusting your course. That is why he changed from his days as a member of the "Gang of Seven" into a very thoughtful legislator. Only one other member of the Gang of Seven amounted to much. Rick Santorum was elected to the Senate twice from Pennsylvania, but was then defeated. He has been running for President every four years since.

Boehner had recently had problems leading his caucus because there were always groups of right-wing Republicans who didn't want him to deal with Democrats. From time to time they mounted efforts to depose him.

As a devout Catholic, Boehner had tried for years to get a Pope to address a joint session of Congress. As Speaker, he was finally able to get Pope Francis to address a joint session of Congress on Sept. 24, 2015. Boehner also had a private session with Pope, who blessed his little granddaughter. It was a historic occasion, because no pope had ever addressed Congress before. The day after Pope Francis did address Congress Speaker Boehner announced that he was resigning both his position as Speaker and his seat in Congress effective October 30.

Unfortunately, it didn't quite happen way he expected. He had groomed a likable young congressman, Kevin McCarthy, to take his place. However McCarthy suddenly backed out because of a rumor among the right wing. I know McCarthy well enough to know that he is a strong family man, so this had to really hurt. Moreover, I don't believe that the rumor was true.

The Republican Party then put pressure on another strong young family man to take the job, Paul Ryan of Wisconsin. He had run unsuccessfully for Vice President with George Romney in 2012, and was serving as Chairman of the House Ways and Means Committee. He initially rejected the offer, but eventually agreed to accept if certain conditions were met. Among these was the understanding that he would not spend a lot of days on the road attending fundraisers for Republican House members as

Boehner had done. Boehner, whose daughters are now in their 30's, had been spending over 200 days a year on the road to help elect Republicans to the House.

Ryan, who is only 45, wanted to spend time with his young family. Moreover, he has never enriched himself while on the public payroll. He still sleeps on a cot in his office and returns home on the weekends.

By this time the party was getting desperate, and even the extremists knew they were painting themselves into a corner. They met Ryan's conditions, and he agreed to be the Speaker of the House. Thus, he was elected Speaker of the House and Boehner was able to step down from his post and resign his seat in the House effective Oct. 30,

Harry Reid and Mitch McConnell

To understand Senator Harry Reid, you must look to the small mining town of Searchlight, Nevada. There in the desert, more than an hour away from the bright lights of Las Vegas, is where he was born and raised.

Searchlight is where Harry Reid watched his father work as a hard rock miner. It's where he attended a school with one teacher for eight grades. Reid is one of only three senators who served eight years as Senate Majority Leader. The others were Alben Barkley and Mike Mansfield. I was a young staff member when the courtly Mike Mansfield was the leader. Reid became leader when my friend Tom Daschle of South Dakota was defeated in his race for reelection.

Daschle was a friend of mine I had known since he was a green young Congressman from South Dakota. He was the leader of the "Gasohol Caucus", as the House members supporting the ethanol industry were known in those days. When he was elected to the Senate in 1986, he began a rapid rise up the ladder to lead his party in the Senate. He got his chance when Senator George Mitchell announced his retirement as Democratic Minority Leader.

In the history of the Senate, only Lyndon B. Johnson had served fewer years than Daschle before being elected to lead his party. I remember that a group of his supporters held a meeting in my office in support of his candidacy to lead his party in the Senate.

Although Daschle served well, he lost to John Thune in his bid for reelection in 2004. The State of South Dakota had become very red, a trend that was begun in 1980 when his old mentor, George McGovern, was defeated in his bid for reelection. Daschle was always a gentleman and kept up on the issues in Agriculture, even though he was busy as Senate Majority Leader. I remember no case where he was harshly partisan in leading the Senate.

Daschle was succeeded by Harry Reid of Nevada, and things took on a more partisan turn in the Senate.

I have nothing personal against Reid. In fact, he worked his way through law school the way that I did, by working on the midnight shift of the Capitol Police Force. He is a couple of years older than I. Moreover, he was already married with children, and I was single. We did not know each other because he worked on the Senate Office Building shift and I worked on the

Capitol Building shift. I only found out that he had worked on the Capitol Police Force only later when I met him at a reception.

In addition to his more partisan tone, I have also noticed his harsh criticism of the Koch brothers. They are rich and conservative political donors. Most, but not all, of their contributions go to Republican members of Congress. However, never before has anyone used their leadership post in Congress to attack private donors to the political parties the way Reid has done the Kochs.

Reid has excoriated them because they donate to conservative political causes and candidates. In the first seven months of 2014, Reid mentioned the Kochs in 22 separate floor speeches, calling them out 250 times. Reid used the term "un-American" to describe the brothers..

"It's too bad that they are trying to buy America. And it's time that the American people spoke out against this terrible dishonesty of these two brothers, who are about as un-American as anyone that I can imagine."

Conservatives, such as MSNBC talk show host Joe Scarborough, compared Reid's comments to "McCarthyism" and National Review editor Rich Lowry condemned Reid's comments.

In 2012, Reid cited fellow U.S. Senator Bernie Sanders, who claimed the Koch brothers were "funding think tanks spreading an enormous amount of disinformation about Social Security". Two years later, in 2014, Reid accused the brothers of having Republicans stall aid to Ukraine by pushing for amendments for a delay of regulation by the IRS of non-profit political advocacy groups. Reid "credited his wife, Landra, for likening the Republicans' Ukrainian stance to a 'Koch addiction".

I also have noticed that Reid led attacks against the Senate Minority Leader, Mitch McConnell. I had never before witnessed such attacks from the leader of one party against a fellow Senator who was the leader of the other party. There was a good reason for this tradition of comity between the two party leaders in the Senate. They knew that when the political battles were over it was then necessary for them to work together to do the business of the people.

In the interest of full disclosure I should say that McConnell and I went to work as young Senate staff members at the same time. I worked as a legislative assistant for a Democratic Senator and he for a Republican Senator Marlowe

Cook. . Neither one of us was the least bit partisan. Our offices were around the corner from each other on the third floor of the Russell Senate Office Building.

Subsequently, I worked my way up as a Counsel and then General Counsel and Staff Director of the Senate Agriculture Committee. McConnell soon returned to Kentucky to practice law and get in politics. He was first elected as County Executive of Louisville County. He then entered a race against Senator Dee Huddleston, who people considered very popular. McConnell seemed to come out of nowhere to defeat Huddleston, who had been up by over 30 points in the polls a few months earlier.

McConnell immediately started working his way up the leadership ladder. He took the job no one wanted, Chairman of the Senate Ethics Committee. Senators don't want this job because they are loathe to pass judgement on their fellow Senators.

Soon after McConnell became chairman, several former female staffers accused Senator Bob Packwood of sexual harassment. Packwood was much his senior and chairman of the most powerful committee in the Senate, the Finance Committee. When McConnell and

I were junior staffers, we were friends of his legislative assistant. In fact, Packwood was revered as having been an author of the Tax Reform Act of 1986. That was in the era when bi-partisanship still ruled.

It was also an era when women were no longer willing to tolerate the sexism and sometimes harassment that used to be winked at in the Senate. In 1991, Clarence Thomas was nominated by President George H. W. Bush for a seat on the Supreme Court to fill the seat of retiring Justice Thurgood Marshall. Unfortunately 'Thomas's career almost was stalled when one of his former aides at the EEOC, Anita Hill, came forward and testified that he had sexually harassed her during the time she worked for him.

While the nation watched Hill's televised testimony with great interest, Thomas then forcefully responded by calling the hearings "a high tech lynching". The Senate decided that there was not enough evidence to prove her claims. Thomas was approved by the Senate by a very small margin, a vote of 52-48

However, the way people view sexual harassment has never been the same. This was demonstrated by what soon happened to none of the most respected members of the Senate.

In 1996, I happened to be listening on the radio when McConnell, as the young Chairman of the Ethics Committee, brought charges against Senator Packwood of Oregon. McConnell had been a friend of the older Senator. However, when McConnell was finished, Packwood had no place to hide.

The Ethics Committee, composed equally of Republican and Democratic senators, voted unanimously to expel Packwood from the Senate. Packwood resigned from the Senate a few days later. Ironically, I remember attending a dinner for Packwood where he lectured our group that the most important new issue was equal rights for women.

When the sexual harassment allegations came to light, Packwood fled to the Hazelden Foundation clinic for alcoholism in Minnesota, claiming that his drinking led to the harassments.

Two years later, during debate on President Clinton's impeachment, McConnell said that the Republicans knew that it was very likely Packwood's seat would fall to the Democrats if Packwood were forced out. However,

McConnell said, he and his fellow Republicans felt the choice was to "retain the Senate seat or retain our honor." Sure enough, the Republicans lost the seat to Democrat Ron Wyden, who is still in the Senate.

McConnell then served as Chairman of the National Republican Senatorial Committee. Republicans maintained control of the Senate in both his terms as chairman. He was first elected as Majority Whip in the 108th Congress and unanimously re-elected on November 17, 2004. In November 2006, after Republicans lost control of the Senate, they elected McConnell to replace Senator Bill Frist as Minority Leader. After Republicans took control of the Senate following the 2014 Senate elections, McConnell became the Senate Majority Leader.

As McConnell worked his way up, he was a centrist or moderate Republican. In later years, McConnell followed his party and became somewhat more conservative. For most of Obama's presidency, McConnell was the face of Republican loyal opposition. Despite McConnell's reputation as a moderate, he said his No. 1 goal was to make Président Obama a one-term President. However, McConnell was at the table when the big deals have been finalized—be they over threats of government shutdowns, debt defaults, or fiscal cliffs. That is the way our two party system is supposed to work.

McConnell had a tough race for reelection to the Senate in 2014. He was first opposed in the Republican primary by a weird tea party candidate, Matt Bevin. When he won the primary the Senate Democratic Campaign Committee under the leadership of Harry Reid had a credible Democratic woman candidate waiting for him. She was well-funded by Hollywood celebrities and had the National Democratic Party raising a very large sum of money for her. What bothered me were the constant attacks against McConnell by Democrat colleagues in the Senate. In times past, one Senator would never directly involve himself in the race against a Senate colleague from another state. This might happen to some limited extent, but not to this extent.

I get constant political appeals and propaganda from both sides of the aisle, but the attacks led by Reid was the worst I have ever seen. It was not only the words, but the physical caricatures were terrible.

In another case where Reid's hand was evident, my old friend Senator Pat Roberts had a tough reelection race in Kansas. However, he was able to defeat a weird tea party opponent in the Republican primary.

In the general election he had a tough race against an "independent" that refused to say which party he would caucus with. It was obvious he had been recruited by the Senate Democratic Leadership under Harry Reid. The Democratic leadership persuaded the legitimate Democratic candidate to withdraw after polls showed him far behind. They then persuaded an "independent" candidate to run in the general election with their support.

Roberts was able to pull out a victory by a ten point margin. However, this race got a lot of national attention because it was thought that control of the Senate could depend on it. As it turned out, that was wrong, because Roberts beat the "independent" and Republicans picked up 9 seats.

Despite the attacks by Reid against McConnell I have not heard McConnell respond in kind since he became Majority Leader in the midterm elections of 2014. While McConnell is a tough negotiator, he does not make it overly partisan. Moreover, he allows votes on the important issues of the day. The new Republican-controlled Senate had already voted on more amendments in one week than the Democratic-controlled Senate considered in all of 2014. Republican senators applauded the feat when Senate Majority Leader Mitch McConnell (R-Ky.) announced it on the Senate floor.

Epilogue

When I look back on a long career that is far from over, I feel lucky. Both in the Senate and in private practice I had a chance to play a key role on issues that changed the world. The first of these was futures and derivatives trading. For more than a century the New York Stock Exchange was the king of the world. It has been gratifying to see that the futures exchanges have taken over the New York Stock Exchange. This has been possible only because we created an obscure little agency, the Commodity Futures Trading Commission, before the SEC was wise to what we were doing.

In the farm policy area, I was fortunate to be in key role in the transition from government controlled and heavily subsidized policies begun by Franklin D Roosevelt in the Great Depression. We built a market system based on the public-private partnership of the Federal Crop Insurance Program. I have been involved since my old friend Secretary of Agriculture Bob Bergland appeared before the Senate Agriculture Committee and testified that, "Our Federal disaster programs are themselves a disaster".

When I entered private practice, I was fortunate enough to be hired by Bland Lee of Old Republic to represent his company on crop insurance issues. He introduced me to Mike Felt, who hired me to be the first Chief Counsel and Executive Director of the American Association of Crop Insurers. I remain in that position today, with a slightly different title. This public private partnership cost the taxpayer much less than the old fixed payment programs.

The third major area is the Federal Checkoff Programs. They reached a new level in 1973 when my old friend Joe Westwater, with some help from me, successfully lobbied for the passage of the Dairy and Tobacco Adjustment Act of 1973. The Dairy Checkoff program is still the largest, but other commodities quickly followed suit. I was able to help the beef and soybean industries establish similar programs, and I drafted the legislation for the Pork Checkoff.

I am proud of all the checkoff programs because they require no government subsidies. As I described previously in this book, none of these reforms would have been possible without the wise stewardship of Secretary Lyng in the Reagan administration.

Lest you think I am just bragging on an unblemished record of winners, I did have one huge disappointment in recent years. My first client was the Chicago Board of Trade, and the second was the United Egg Producers (UEP). When I was hired by them, they were only a federation of four regional cooperatives. The real power (and budget control) was in the regional CEOs. Consequently, UEP seemed to always be broke. I would often work for months without being paid, and their Washington office was run out of my law offices. I was able to do this because my main client was the Chicago Board of Trade.

Over the years I worked with the CEO, Al Pope, to create a trade association, the United Egg Association (UEA) that brought in funds from the further processing and the allied industry sectors of the industry. Even more important, we were able to develop a substantial political action committee called EggPac. Without one, it is hard for any trade association to be effective.

Everything turned bad when the industry was confronted with the animal activist lobby, principally the Humane Society of the US (HSUS). In an attempt to placate the activists UEP adopted a new humane standard called UEP Certified. This effort caused the trade association and its members to be sued for anti-trust violations. Eventually, this law suit cost the industry over $100 million.

All this took place as my old friend Al Pope was being forced out of the CEO position, and another man who he had hired had taken over. The situation got worse when California passed a law that required caged chickens be given more space. Despite mounting a public relations effort that cost the industry $10 million, the industry lost by a two to one margin.

UEP panicked and cut a deal with its enemy. In a much hyped deal in which I was excluded from involvement, the UEP reached, without counsel, a grand bargain with the vegan HSUS. It was elaborately staged, with management urging that the former chairman of the Democratic Party in Iowa be paid $5 million to cut a deal with Secretary Vilsack. Fortunately, some of the Board from Ohio had bad experiences with this guy. The UEP Board met with this operative in my office and refused to pay him. Also, Vilsack refused to even acknowledge that he knew the Iowa lawyer who tried this scheme.

I tried to dissuade the UEP management from this reckless course, and even took them in to see my friend Collin Peterson, then Chairman of the House Agriculture Committee. They asked him his opinion, and he said he was strongly opposed. They asked what he would do if they went ahead with it, and he said, "If I see you are getting anywhere, I will just have to kill it."

Despite this warning, I could not bring myself to desert a client I had strong ties with almost my entire career, going back to the time I was a public servant on the Senate Agriculture Committee staff. I had to fight Carol Tucker Forman in her efforts to have the government stop people from eating eggs.

This did cause a member of my staff to leave the law firm and get out of lobbying all together rather than lobby for such an unpopular cause. It is interesting that he is again working for UEP now that the egg bill is gone.

Finally, after 2 years' efforts, it became evident that our egg bill would never be passed as a part of the 2014 farm bill. I persuaded the client to cut their losses and drop it (or so I thought). UEP then had their annual meeting at the Biltmore Estate. I went about trying to heal the fissures that had been created by UEP management.

I noticed that I was excluded from any board meetings where decisions were made. Two people tried to warn me. One was my friend Amon Baer, who had led an organization opposed to management's disastrous course of action. Another was my wife, who has good instincts about these things.

Shortly thereafter the meeting was over and the UEP members went home. Then the management had their general counsel inform me I was fired and that I should return their files. This was the first time I had been fired from anything in my entire life. They also fired Mitch Head of Golin Harris, their long time public relations man, the best PR man I ever knew.

My only regret is I did not withdraw earlier, when I knew this was wrong. It is the only thing I am ashamed of in my entire long career. It endangered our representation of other segments of animal agriculture, which were a lot more important to my law firm than the egg industry. Ultimately, it would have impaired the firm's representation of the dairy industry and the representation of the rest of animal agriculture. Moreover, it would not have worked even if we had passed the egg bill. There are many other animal activist groups besides HSUS who are now forcing the industry to go completely cage free.

Currently, I am counseling on a pro bono basis a little start-up organization, the National Association of Egg Farmers. It is headed by one of the most ethical guys I know, Ken Klippen. He had been chosen by Al Pope to be his heir apparent, after having served as the CEO of the International Egg Commission and as the chief Washington lobbyist of UEP. However he was forced out by the current UEP management.

I never want to represent the egg industry again.

But hey---I don't want to end this book on a down note! Every day, as I do my morning run, I say a little prayer thanking God for the privilege of living in the greatest country in the history of the world. Also, I am thankful that I am in perfect health.

Where else could a poor boy that grew up on a little farm in nowhere, South Georgia have had such mentors as Senator Talmadge, Vice President Humphrey, and Senate Majority Leader Byrd? I feel both privileged and lucky. They taught me that I too could make a difference.

With all of the wars we have had in my life time, some ill-conceived by our Presidents, we will still prevail in the end. We have to. We are the last best hope for mankind. We are still "the Shining City on the Hill".

Appendix

Herman Talmadge was my first role model and is more responsible than anyone for whatever success I have achieved in life. He taught me to be prompt and honest in all my professional dealings. Most important, he taught me to be loyal. That is why I have always believed that anyone who is disloyal is no damned good. He was like a father to me and said that I was like a son to him in a going away party the he hosted when I left him for private practice in 1978.

Also, I saw an example of this in a young friend of Talmadge. There was a young tax lawyer from Oklahoma named JD Williams. He had come to Washington as an aide to the powerful Oklahoma Senator Bob Kerr. However Kerr died in1963. JD then worked in the losing presidential campaign of Hubert Humphrey in I968.

Despite having to start at the bottom, JD became the most successful lobbyist of his time. He did so by following a very simple philosophy, "to have a friend be a friend ". He followed this code faithfully, whether it was serving as the best man for me in my first wedding or in representing congressmen who were subject to actions in court. His firm Williams and Jenson is still successful today.

I will always have a sense of remorse regarding Talmadge. When his office chief of staff, Bo Ginn, went back to Georgia to run for Congress, Talmadge offered me the job. However, I wanted to be known as a lawyer, not as a political operative. I chose to remain as the General Counsel and Chief of Staff of the Senate Agriculture Committee.

One reason I made this choice was that I remembered the advice of Joe Bowman, who represented the Chicago Board of Trade when its president was Henry Hall Wilson. Joe said, "Son, don't you ever give up the practice of law in your work in the Senate." Bowman soon died and was buried with full military honors in a funeral I attended for Talmadge in the Arlington National Memorial Cemetery. His words had a huge impact on me.

Talmadge was undone by a series of personal tragedies I would not have believed. His son and my friend, Bobby Talmadge, an avid water skier, died while swimming in a lake in 1975.. Bobby and I had been good friends, and we double dated one summer when I was stationed in Atlanta. Bobby left his young wife, Lyniece, and a daughter and son behind.

This tragedy triggered a breach in Herman's marriage of many years and drove him to excessive drinking. I had been with Talmadge and his wife, Betty, frequently, and I had always noticed that they had a loving relationship. He always called her "Honey." However, the loss of their son Bobby destroyed this loving relationship, and eventually Talmadge filed for divorce. As they say, "Hell hath no fury like a woman scorned." Subsequently, I have known of other cases where the death of a child has caused a great strain, and sometimes a divorce, in a marriage.

Betty was the first person to publicly accuse Talmadge of financial improprieties, and her allegations were avidly published in the Atlanta newspapers. This prompted an investigation by the Senate Ethics Committee. She then testified against him at the hearings before the Senate Ethics Committee.

Her most famous charge was that he kept wads of hundred-dollar bills in overcoats in their coat closet. Having spent time in both of their homes, the one in Washington and the one in Lovejoy, Georgia, I knew that was a lie. In Lovejoy, the doors of the house were never locked and people could come and go at will. She loved money more than he did, and she would never have allowed one hundred dollar bills to lie around that way.

This charge would later become the basis of campaign ads run by his political opponent in his next election. Ironically, this charge was made by Norman Underwood, who had been my friend at the University of Georgia Law School. He is the one who first gave me the idea of working for Talmadge. He had earlier served as a "patronage boy" for Senator Russell.

When I declined Talmadge's offer of the job of his chief of staff, I recommended that he consider two other young friends of mine from Georgia whom I held in high regard. One was Dan Minchew, a guy I had shared a house with after I began work on Talmadge's staff. The other was George Watts, a University of Georgia graduate who had served as chief of staff for a South Georgia congressman.

I first met Minchew when he was the president of the Georgia 4-H Club. Later, I was impressed by him because he had gone to school in Oxford, England, after he graduated from the University of Georgia. He was the president of the Oxford Club in Washington, which met in the house we shared on Capitol Hill.

After interviewing both men and calling his friends in Georgia, Talmadge chose Minchew. He served as Talmadge's office chief of staff, and subsequently as of the Chairman of the International Trade Commission. He obtained that position only because of Talmadge's support. When Betty Talmadge made her public charges against her husband, it prompted an investigation by the Senate Ethics Committee.

The Senate Ethics Committee staff conducted an investigation of Talmadge's office accounts, and that formed the basis of public hearings. They found a shortfall of $43,435. They also examined the books of the Senate Agriculture Committee, which I was responsible for, just as Minchew was responsible for the accounts in his personal office. They found nothing improper in the Senate Agriculture Committee books.

The IRS then conducted an investigation of the case and found nothing wrong on the part of Talmadge. However, the IRS found criminal fraud on the part of Minchew, who was sentenced to prison and served hard time. It turned out that he was deeply in debt to old friends because of his real estate speculation on Capitol Hill. He committed larceny to stay afloat. The fraud conviction and jail time caused

Minchew to lose everything. He is now working as a travel guide in Washington.

During Herman's messy divorce from Betty, the details of his financial holdings became public. The disclosures of Talmadge's great wealth caused a lot of speculation that he had done something wrong. However, his wealth came from two things.

First, his father left him the largest tract of undeveloped land south of Atlanta, some three thousand acres. Talmadge developed it and made a World War II veteran, Winsor Daniel, wealthy by having him build the houses. He named this posh Development Talmadge Lake. It was one of the few things a public official could do without a conflict of interest.

Second, he was an astute investor in the stock market. After his forced retirement, I would visit him in his little house in Lovejoy house near Talmadge Lake on the property (Betty had taken the old family mansion from him in their divorce settlement). He would be watching the financial channels on TV and he would be trading stocks full blast. He told me he was making a fortune trading bank stocks.

Much later, I would follow his example and build vacation rental houses around a little lake in my forty acre development next to the Blue Ridge Parkway in Asheville, NC. Also, I found that I was a pretty good stock picker myself, although not as good as he. I go running and walking over my forty acres early every morning that I am home just as he did over his three thousand acres. That is when I still think of him.

Unfortunately, his heirs would fight over his estate for over a decade after his death. This was despite the fact that Talmadge hired one of the best estate lawyers in Atlanta to plan and administer his estate.

Unfortunately, the publicity from these personal tragedies resulted in Talmadge's narrow defeat in his 1980 election, the same one in which Jimmy Carter was defeated by Ronald Reagan.

After his forced retirement, I remained his friend and visitor until his death over 20 years later. At his funeral in March, 2002 I was glad to see President Carter was sitting on the front row of the church.